URBANIZATION AND RURAL DYNAMICS IN INDIA

POPULATION, POLICIES, AND PERSPECTIVES

DR ANSHUMALI PANDEY

DR VIVEK SIDHU

Contents

Preface

It is with great pleasure that we present this book, "Urbanization and Rural Dynamics in India: Population, Policies, and Perspectives." This work delves into the complex and multifaceted interplay between urbanization and rural development in the Indian context, exploring the various factors that shape and are shaped by these dynamics. The aim of this book is to provide a comprehensive understanding of the demographic, economic, and institutional landscapes that define contemporary India.

India, with its vast and diverse population, presents a unique case study for examining the impacts of urbanization on rural areas and vice versa. The chapters of this book are designed to cover a wide array of topics that are critical to understanding these dynamics.

1. **Population**: This chapter provides an overview of India's population trends, including growth patterns, distribution, and demographic characteristics. It sets the stage for understanding the subsequent discussions on urbanization and rural development.
2. **Urbanization**: Here, we explore the process of urbanization in India, examining its causes, patterns, and consequences. The chapter highlights the challenges and opportunities that urban growth presents to both urban and rural areas.
3. **Tribal Areas**: This chapter focuses on the unique demographic and socio-economic characteristics of India's tribal regions. It discusses the impacts of urbanization and development policies on these communities, emphasizing the need for inclusive and culturally sensitive approaches.
4. **Population Problems and Policies**: In this section, we delve into the issues arising from India's population dynamics, such as overpopulation, migration, and the demographic dividend. The chapter also reviews the various policies implemented to address these challenges.
5. **Agricultural Infrastructure**: Recognizing the critical role of agriculture in India's rural economy, this chapter examines the state of agricultural infrastructure. It discusses the improvements needed to enhance productivity and ensure sustainable rural development.
6. **Institutional Factors**: This chapter explores the role of various institutions, including government agencies, non-governmental

organizations, and local bodies, in shaping rural and urban development. It highlights the importance of effective governance and institutional support in driving positive change.

7. **Industrial Scenario**: The final chapter looks at the industrial landscape of India, analyzing the impact of industrialization on rural and urban areas. It considers the balance between industrial growth and the need for sustainable development practices.

Through these chapters, "Urbanization and Rural Dynamics in India" aims to provide a holistic understanding of the interconnections between population, policies, and development perspectives. It is my hope that this book will serve as a valuable resource for students, researchers, policymakers, and anyone interested in the intricate dynamics of India's urban and rural landscapes.

We would like to extend our gratitude to all those who have contributed to this work, and we hope that this book will inspire further research and discussion on these vital issues.

Dr. Anshumali Pandey
Dr Vivek Sidhu

Prologue

The story of India's development is a tale of contrasts and convergences, where urbanization and rural dynamics intersect in complex and often unpredictable ways. This book, "Urbanization and Rural Dynamics in India: Population, Policies, and Perspectives," embarks on a journey to unravel these intricate connections, providing readers with a comprehensive understanding of how India's population trends, economic transformations, and policy landscapes interact to shape the nation's future.

As we step into the 21st century, India stands at a critical juncture. The rapid pace of urbanization has brought about significant changes in the social, economic, and environmental fabric of the country. Cities are expanding, driven by the influx of people seeking better opportunities and living conditions. Yet, this urban growth presents numerous challenges, including the need for sustainable infrastructure, equitable resource distribution, and the preservation of cultural heritage.

Simultaneously, India's rural areas are undergoing profound transformations. The traditional agrarian lifestyle is being reshaped by technological advancements, policy interventions, and market forces. Rural communities are increasingly becoming integrated into the larger economic framework, yet they face persistent challenges such as inadequate infrastructure, limited access to education and healthcare, and the pressures of out-migration.

This book is structured to provide a detailed exploration of these themes, starting with the foundational aspects of India's population dynamics. It then delves into the phenomenon of urbanization, highlighting both its drivers and its repercussions. The focus on tribal areas underscores the diversity and unique challenges faced by some of India's most marginalized communities.

The discussion on population problems and policies offers insights into the demographic challenges and the strategies devised to address them. Agricultural infrastructure, a cornerstone of rural development, is examined in depth, revealing the gaps and opportunities for enhancing productivity and sustainability. The role of institutional factors is scrutinized to understand how governance and policy frameworks influence development outcomes.

Finally, the industrial scenario is analyzed to provide a comprehensive view of how industrialization impacts both urban and rural settings, balancing economic growth with environmental and social considerations.

I invite readers to embark on this intellectual journey, exploring the nuanced and interconnected aspects of India's development. This book aims to be more than just an academic exercise; it is a call to action for policymakers, scholars, and citizens to engage with the critical issues at hand and work towards a more balanced and inclusive future for India.

Dr. Anshumali Pandey

CHAPTER ONE

POPULATIONS

INTRODUCTION

Population is the basic element of a state or a nation— it provides skilled manpower that can be geared towards the economic development of the country. The strength and progress of any nation resides in the quality of its population— educated, healthy and hardworking people contribute to the betterment and advancement of the country.

In terms of population, India is the second most populous country in world, only led by People's Republic of China. With a total population of approximately 121 crore (Census 2011), India contributes to about 17% of the total world population. However, this enormous population inhabits only 2.4% area of the world, thereby causing an intense pressure on land and natural resources. This in turn creates a number of economic and social issues such as low standards of living and education, poverty and malnourishment. The ever-increasing population of India is also advancing a threat to the progress of the country, as the poverty and illiteracy rates rise with the rise in population.

In this unit, we present the population profile in India (as per Census of India 2011) by focusing on the population distribution, density, growth and composition. We will also discuss the differences in population trends in rural and urban setting, and the factors that are likely influencing the distribution and growth of population in India.

DISTRIBUTION OF POPULATION

A number of natural and cultural factors control distribution of Population. Though scholars put more weight on the natural factors, however, scholars *Clarke* and *Zelinsky* maintain that the cultural factors are more significant in determining the concentration and distribution of population in any given region. Furthermore, according to *Clarke and Zelinsky*, progressive development of the region, which is dependent on economic and social conditions, technological development and government policy plays a vital role in the distribution of the population.

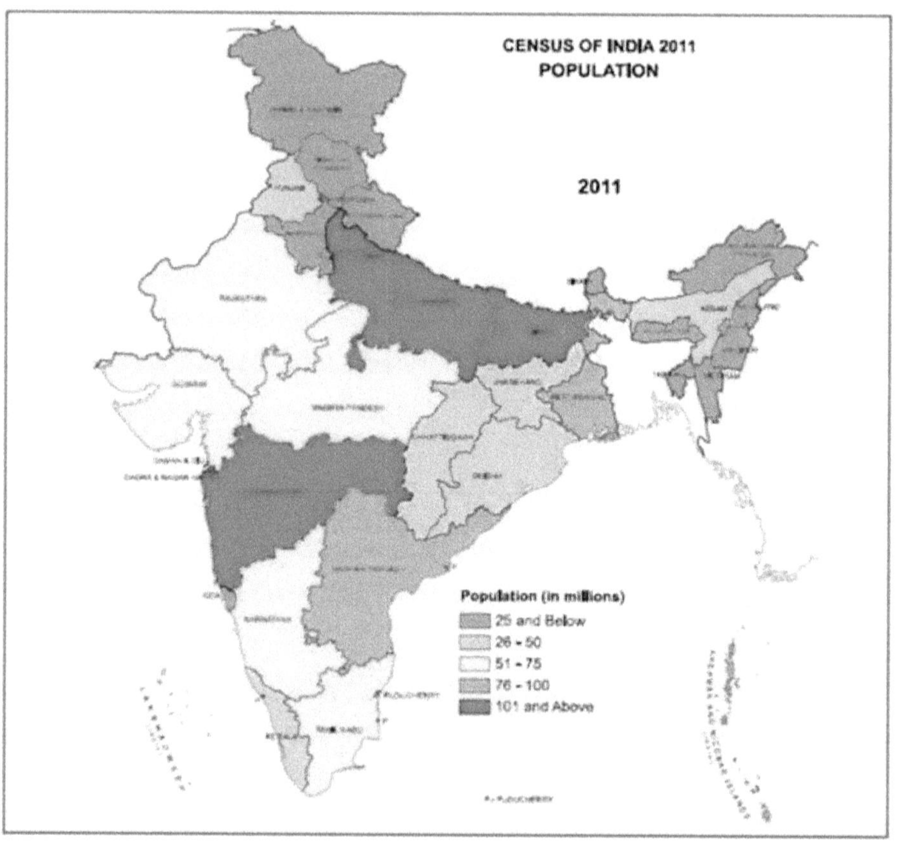

Fig 1.1: State wise Population distribution in India*Source: Census of India 2011*

Table 1.1 State wise Population and Percent Decadal Change

State (U.Ts. denoted by *)	Population (in millions) (2011)	% Decadal Change (2001 - 2011)
INDIA	**1,210,193,422**	17.64
Andaman & Nicobar Is. *	379,944	6.68
Andhra Pradesh	84,665,533	11.10
Arunachal Pradesh	1,382,611	25.92
Assam	31,169,272	16.93
Bihar	103,804,637	25.07
Chandigarh *	1,054,686	17.10
Chattishgarh	25,540,196	22.59
Dadra & Nagar Haveli *	342,853	55.50
Daman & Diu *	242,911	53.54
Delhi *	16,753,235	20.96
Goa	1,457,723	8.17
Gujrat	60,383,628	19.17
Haryana	25,353,081	19.90
Himachal Pradesh	6,856,509	12.81
Jammu & Kashmir	12,548,926	23.71
Jharkhand	32,966,238	22.34
Karnataka	61,130,704	15.67
Kerela	33,387,677	4.86
Lakshadweep *	64,429	6.23
Madhya Pradesh	72,597,565	20.30
Maharashtra	112,372,972	15.99
Manipur	2,721,756	18.65
Meghalaya	2,964,007	27.82
Mizoram	1,091,014	22.78
Nagaland	1,980,602	-0.47
Odisha	41,947,358	13.97
Puducherry *	1,244,464	27.72
Punjab	27,704,236	13.73
Rajasthan	68,621,012	21.44
Sikkim	607,688	12.36
Tamil Nadu	72,138,958	15.60
Tripura	3,671,032	14.75
Uttar Pradesh	199,581,477	20.09
Uttarakhand	10,116,752	19.17
West Bengal	91,347,736	13.93

Source: Census of India 2011 (Provisional Population Totals, Paper I of 2011—Series I)

The distribution of population in India is highly unequal. The most populous states are Maharashtra, Uttar Pradesh, Bihar, Andhra Pradesh and West Bengal, and accounts for almost 50% of the population of India. Whereas, the hilly states in the north-east, and the northern states of Jammu and Kashmir, Himachal Pradesh and Uttarakhand account for some of the lowest populations (contributing to only about 4% to the total population of India). Daman and Diu, Dadra and Nagar Haveli and the islands of Lakshadweep, are some of least populated states (UT) in India.

On the district level, Thane district of Maharashtra has the highest population (approx. 1.11 crore), while Dibang Valley of Arunachal Pradesh is least population consisting of only about 8000 people. City wise, the urban metropolitan cities of Mumbai, Delhi, Bangalore, Hyderabad and Ahmedabad are the top five populous cities. Mumbai and Delhi, both host a population of more than 1 crore. The urbanization factor and the educational factors are the most important factors which play a huge role in this kind of population in these cities. A more progressive and developed area with more opportunities for employment, variety of sources of entertainment and affordable standards of living tends to attract a higher number of population.

POPULATION GROWTH

Though the estimates of population in India are available since late 1700's, the first consensus was undertaken in 1871. Up until 1901, the growth rate was very slow, varying between 0.09% and 1.1% per annum. According to the famous American sociologist Kingslay Davis, "India's population remained almost stationary since 1800 at around 125 million for about 50 years. The population recorded at the time of 1881 census exceeded the figure for 1921 by only 1.47 crores." The reason for the slow population growth rate was the increased mortality rate due to famines, plagues and other epidemics.

The population growth rate since 1901-2011 shows 3 distinct phases: stagnant population (1901-1921); steadily increasing population (1921-1951) and rapidly growing population from (1951-2011).

Table 1.2 Growth of Population in India from 1901 to 2011

Year	Population (millions)	Decadal Change (%)	Average Annual Growth rate (%)
1901	238.3	—	—
1911	252.0	+5.75	0.56
1921	251.2	-0.31	-0.03
1931	278.9	+11.00	1.04
1941	318.6	+14.22	1.33
1951	361.0	+13.22	1.25
1961	439.2	+21.51	1.96
1971	548.1	+24.80	2.20
1981	683.3	+24.66	2.22
1991	844.3	+23.50	2.14
2001	1027.0	+21.54	1.97
2011	1210.0	+17.64	1.64

Source: Census of India 2011

The stagnant population phase, continued from the 1800's to early 1900's. The population from 1901-1921 witnessed a stagnant population, increasing from about 238 million in 1901 to about 251 million 1921, resulting in an average growth rate of 0.27% per annum. From 1911- 1921, there is a decline in the population of approximately 1.2 million, mainly due the very high mortality rate because of widespread influenza and extensive famines and drought conditions. The year of 1921 is acknowledged as the "Demographic Divide" between the period of stagnant or fluctuating growth and the period marked by steady population growth from1921 to 1951, the **steady population growth phase**, the population increased by 43.67% from 251 million to 361 million. The main reason for this change in trend of the population growth was that the improved medical facilities, communication, transportation and food production could arrest the growth of mortality due to famines and other epidemics. In the most recent years, the year 1951 marked yet another "**Demographic Divide**" in the growth history of India's population. At this stage, a tremendous amount of increase was witnessed: the country's population increased by approximately 284% between 1951- 2011.

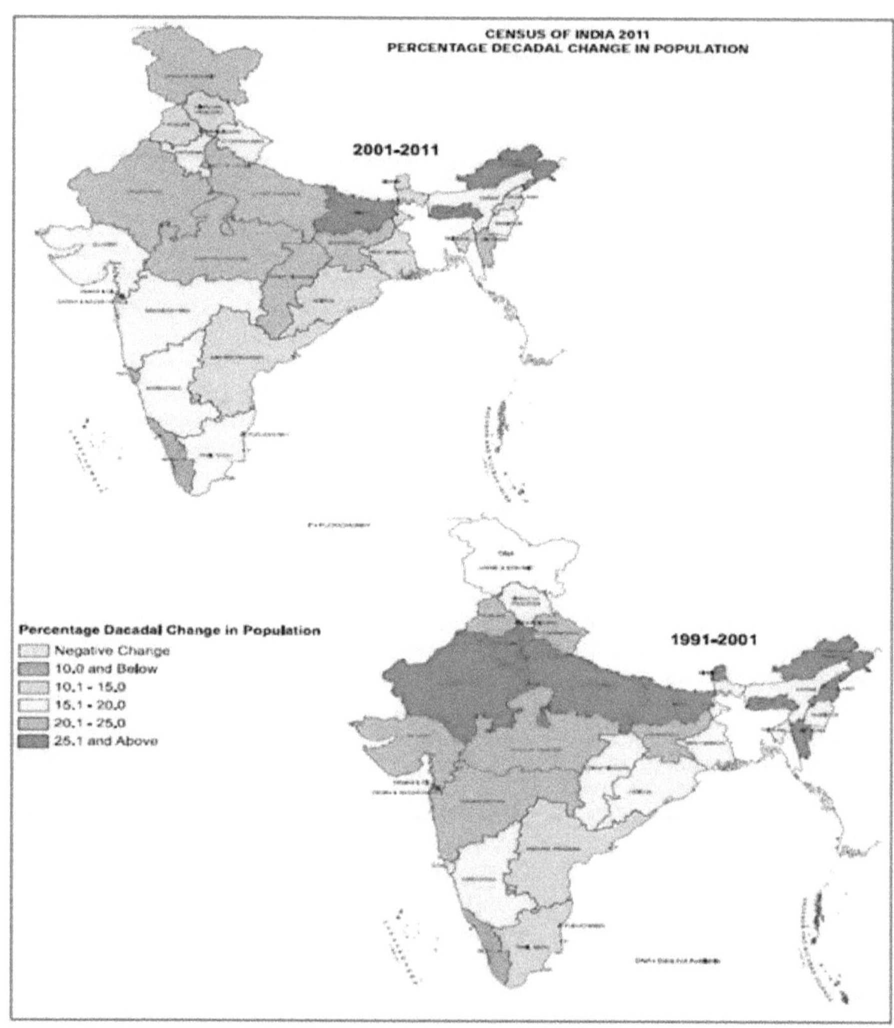

Fig. 1.2 Growth of Population in India*Source: Census of India*

The average annual growth rate by the decades fluctuated between 1.65% and 2.22% per annum. The large scale rapid development, improved medical facilities and increased food production all contributed to lower the mortality rate, along with increasing the birth rate in India. This primarily caused the population to balloon in the recent history of India.

RURAL URBAN DIFFERENCES

Urbanization is the migration of population from not very well developed rural areas such as villages to well-developed urban areas such as cities. This gradual or rapid increase in the proportion of people living in urban areas, cause cities to grow physically as well. This dynamic and evolving nature of the rural-urban makeup of the population reflects the evolution of occupation structure and the state of economy in the nation.

The urban population in 1901 was only about 10.8% of the total population of India, but has been steadily growing from 1951 till present. In the past decade, the urban population has increased from 27.8% to 31.2%. Urbanization in India is not very high as compared to other developing countries. For example, in 2001, the rate of urbanization was 40% for developing countries, about 36% for China, and 33 % for Pakistan. Compared to these, India only had about 27.8%.The degree of urbanization is dependent on the ratio of urban population to total population. States and UT's have been divided into 5 categories based on urbanization (data in Table 1.3):

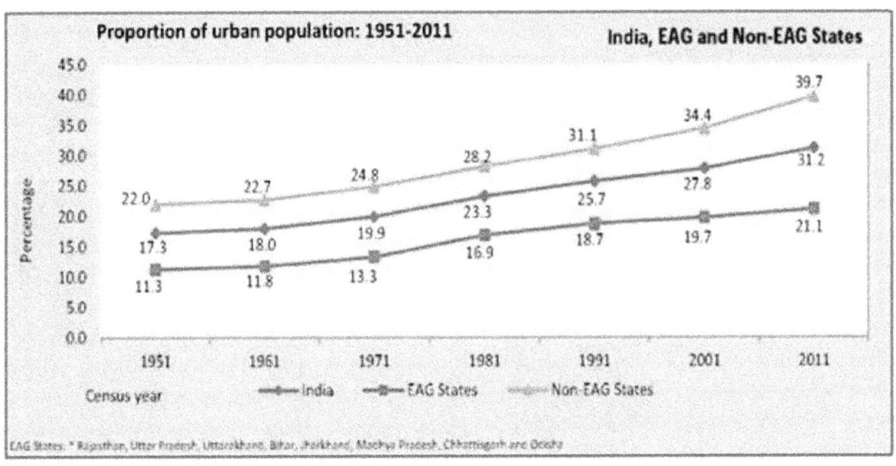

Fig. 1.3 Urbanization trend in India*Source: Census of India, 2011*

i. **very high** (> 60% urbanization) - Delhi, Chandigarh, Puducherry (examples)
ii. **high (40-60%)** - Lakshadweep, Goa, Mizoram, Tamil Nadu, Maharashtra
iii. **high-medium** (30-40%) - Gujarat, Karnataka, Punjab, Haryana, West Bengal, Daman & Diu
iv. **low-medium** (20-30%) - Andhra Pradesh, Uttar Pradesh, Uttarakhand, Kerala, Chhattisgarh
v. **low** (< 20 %) - Assam, Bihar, Sikkim, Himachal Pradesh.

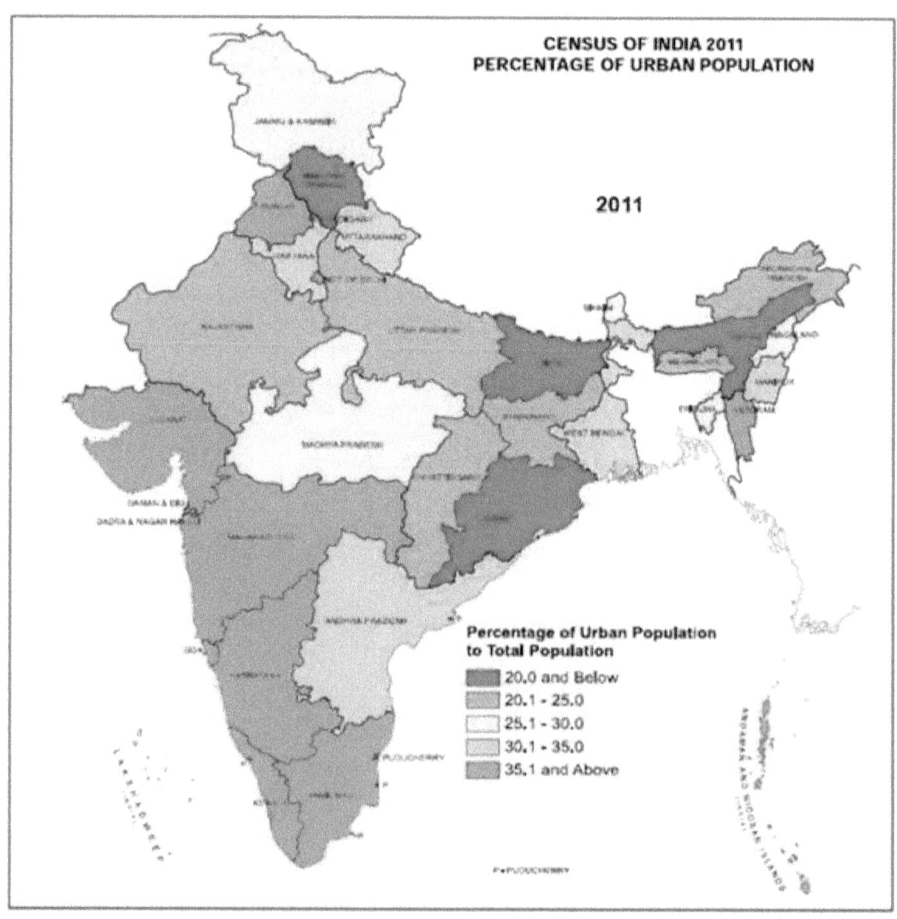

Fig. 1.4 Percentage of Urban Population in India*Source: Census of India, 2011*

Table 1.3 Degree of Urbanization by States

State (U.Ts. denoted by *)	% Urban Population (2001)	% Urban Population (2011)
INDIA	27.8	31.2
Andaman & Nicobar Is. *	32.6	37.7
Andhra Pradesh	27.3	33.4
Arunachal Pradesh	20.8	22.9
Assam	12.9	14.1
Bihar	10.5	11.3
Chandigarh *	89.8	97.3
Chattishgarh	20.1	23.2
Dadra & Nagar Haveli *	22.9	46.7
Daman & Diu *	36.2	75.2
Delhi *	93.2	97.5
Goa	49.8	62.2
Gujrat	37.4	42.6
Haryana	28.9	34.9
Himachal Pradesh	9.8	10.0
Jammu & Kashmir	24.8	27.4
Jharkhand	22.2	24.0
Karnataka	34.0	38.7
Kerela	26.0	47.7
Lakshadweep *	44.5	78.1
Madhya Pradesh	26.5	27.6
Maharashtra	42.4	45.2
Manipur	26.6	32.5
Meghalaya	19.6	20.1
Mizoram	49.6	52.1
Nagaland	17.2	28.9
Odisha	15.0	16.7
Puducherry *	66.6	68.3
Punjab	33.9	37.5
Rajasthan	23.4	24.9
Sikkim	11.1	25.2
Tamil Nadu	44.0	48.4
Tripura	17.1	26.2
Uttar Pradesh	20.8	22.3
Uttarakhand	25.7	30.2
West Bengal	28.0	31.9

Source: *Primary Census Abstract — Data Highlights, Census of India 2011*

DENSITY OF POPULATION

Population density is the measure of persons inhabiting a unit area of land. For example, the population density of India in 2011 was calculated to be 382 persons per square km. The density of population can be seen as a measure of the pressure or strain that a population puts on land resources in a country or a nation. Table 6.4 shows that population density of India from 1901 - 2011. Though the absolute increase in the density has becoming more and more over the decades, the percentage increase has slowed downed. The percentage increase climbed sharply in 1921-1931, and continued to grow steadily until 1961, after which it stabilized in low 20%'s. In the most recent decades, from 1991-2011, the percentage increase shows a decline, from 23.6% to 17.5%. Nevertheless, the population density of India is high and is of concern. The high density puts an immense pressure on available land resources, infrastructure facilities, and therefore, adversely affects the quality of life and environment.

Table 1.4 Density Population (per sq. km) of India (1901 - 2011)

Year	Population Density	Absolute Increase	% Increase
1901	77	—	—
1911	82	5	6.5
1921	81	-1	-1.2
1931	90	9	11.1
1941	103	13	14.4
1951	117	14	13.6
1961	142	25	21.4
1971	177	35	24.6
1981	216	39	22.0
1991	267	51	23.6
2001	325	58	21.7
2011	382	57	17.5

Source: Provisional Population Totals, Paper I of 2011 (Series I)

In India, variation in the spatial pattern of the population density is observed. The population density of each state in 2001 and 2011 is show in Table 1.5 and Density population Maps shown below also serve to distinguish between densely populated areas (Bihar, Delhi, West Bengal) and areas with low population density (Rajasthan, Uttarakhand, Himachal Pradesh).

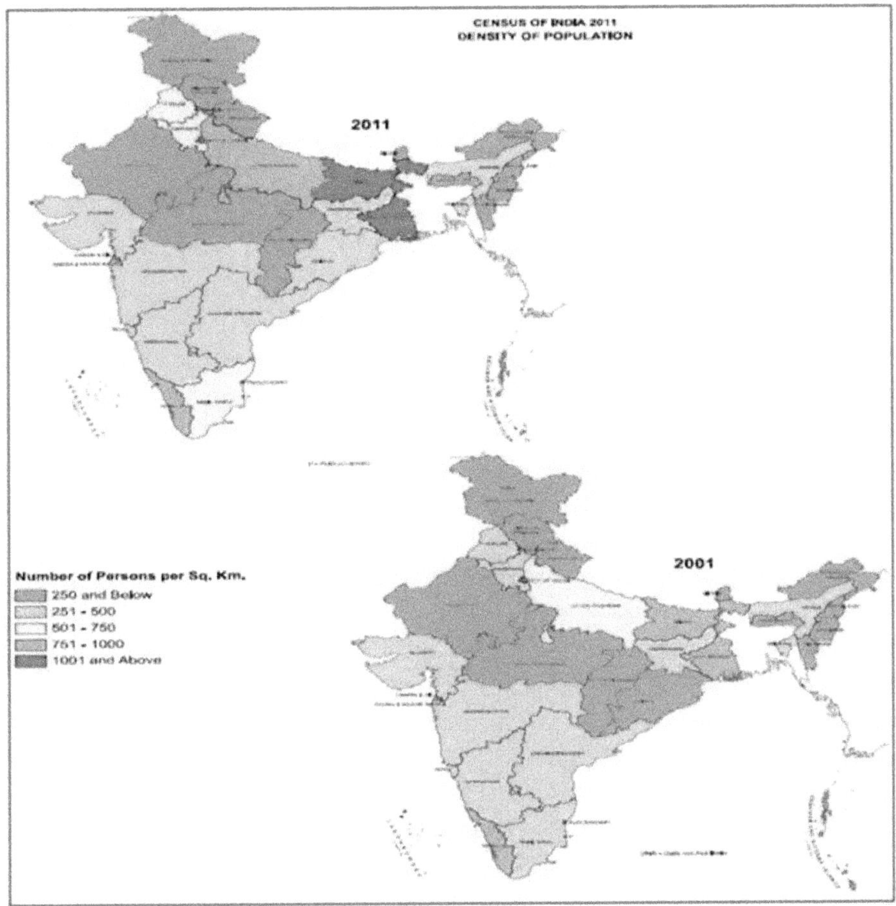

Fig. 1.5 State wise population density of India*Source: Census of India*

Table 1.5 Population Density (per sq. km) by State

State (U.Ts. denoted by *)	2001	2011
INDIA	**352**	**382**
Andaman & Nicobar Is. *	43	46
Andhra Pradesh	277	308
Arunachal Pradesh	13	17
Assam	340	398
Bihar	881	1106
Chandigarh *	7900	9258
Chattishgarh	154	189
Dadra & Nagar Haveli *	449	700
Daman & Diu *	1425	2191
Delhi *	9340	11320
Goa	364	394
Gujrat	258	308
Haryana	478	573
Himachal Pradesh	109	123
Jammu & Kashmir	100	124
Jharkhand	338	414
Karnataka	276	319
Kerela	820	860
Lakshadweep *	2022	2149
Madhya Pradesh	196	236
Maharashtra	315	365
Manipur	97	115
Meghalaya	103	132
Mizoram	42	52
Nagaland	120	119
Odisha	236	270
Puducherry *	1989	2547
Punjab	484	551
Rajasthan	165	200
Sikkim	76	86
Tamil Nadu	480	555
Tripura	305	350
Uttar Pradesh	690	829
Uttarakhand	159	189
West Bengal	903	1028

Source: Primary Census Abstract — Data Highlights, Census of India 2011

FACTORS INFLUENCING DISTRIBUTION OF POPULATION

India, similar to many other developing nations around the world, suffer from over population caused by the rapid population growth rate (approximately 2% per annum) in the recent history of the country, as birth rate continue to tremendously exceed the death rate. The immense population in India is not uniformly distributed and as mentioned in the earlier sections, and distribution of population is controlled by a number of natural and cultural factors. Better employment prospects and higher quality of life leads to difference in the populations of different areas. People migrate to areas offering them a better prospect of life.

Migration is the movement of people from one place to another temporarily or permanently and is composed of four types: rural to rural, rural to urban, urban to rural and urban to urban.

Migration to and from any area primarily influences the distribution of the population in the region. The main causes of migration are economic factors, but factors like marriage, social insecurity, political disturbances, and inter-ethnic conflicts also contribute to migrations. Social factors such as recreation, health care, education, legal services are also a cause for short time migrations. In the cases of males, the disparity in economic development seems to be the main cause of migration. However, in cases of females, marriage is the main cause of migration.

Migration is a product of the "pull" and "push" factors. When it is caused by the attraction of a city, it is attributed to the "pull" factor. Whereas, factors such as unemployment, hunger, and conflicts that cause migration are the "push" factors. Densely populated rural areas with an increased pressure on land resources contribute to outward migration. In big cities, more employment opportunities, plantation agriculture, and Green revolutions seem to be the major "pull" factors in migrations. Rajasthan, Uttar Pradesh, Bihar, Andhra Pradesh and Kerala are major out-migration states. West Bengal, Maharashtra, Assam, Delhi and Chandigarh are mostly in-migration States and Union Territories.

The distribution of population is also determined by the location of resource regions. **Resource Regions** are the regions that have big industrial ad urban clusters with significant scientific and technological resource potential to attract more population. For examples, resource region such as the West Bengal Deltaic Region has a significant pulling affect over the rural population. The Hugli industrial region, the Damodar industrial region and the Deccan region has also attracted a significant amount of in-migrating population. The growth of various industries, widespread urbanization and development of transport facilities, power, education quality etc. in cities such as Ahmedabad, Surat, Nagpur, etc. has also attracted populations from neighborhood areas.

Though urbanization and well developed areas tend to attract populations, the populations are turning away from areas with lesser facilities. For example, the hilly areas of north western Himalayas (Uttarakhand, Himachal Pradesh), eastern hills and plateau and Andaman-Nicobar Islands have rough terrain and poor land resources for practicing agriculture. In addition to that, lack of stable infrastructure has limited the use of other natural resources such as hydro, forest and minerals in these areas. In higher altitudes of these states, the cold temperatures, insufficient food production and meager opportunities for employment further serve as push factors, causing populations to migrate to areas with much favorable living conditions.

All these factors have resulted in a varied distribution pattern of population in India. These factors have led to the most populous states being Maharashtra, Uttar Pradesh, Bihar, Andhra Pradesh and West Bengal, and accounting for almost 50% of the population of India. The unfavorable living conditions for people in the hilly states (Jammu and Kashmir, Himachal Pradesh and Uttarakhand) have led to some of the lowest populations in the country, contributing to only about 4% to the total population of India.

POPULATION COMPOSITION BY AGE, SEX, LITERACY & OCCUPATION STRUCTURE

Population composition refers to the combined demographic characteristics of persons within a country or nation. These characteristics, such as age, sex, and literacy and occupation structure create a profile of the population. Furthermore, these attributes gives the population, its character: whether it is female-dominated, composed mostly of senior citizens or has a below average literacy rate. Population composition of an area can be useful when predicting the heath service demands, energy consumption and other socio-economic factors. This in turn can be useful while implementing government policies and allotting development funds in the region. Here we present India's demographic based on age, sex, literacy, and occupation structure.

AGE STRUCTURE

The age structure of a population is an important factor in population dynamics and evolution. Age structure is the proportion of a population in different age groups (Table 1.6). Age structure is one of the most important factors in determining the proportion working population available that can contribute to the labor force and the dependent population in the total population. Population models that incorporate age structure in its criteria make better prediction of population growth, plus enhance the ability to associate this growth with the level of economic development in a region, thereby also aiding in the making of development policies

Over the course of history in India, the working population (in the age group 15-60) constitutes about 50-55% of the total population of India, the remaining being the dependent population (0-14 age group and 60 & above age group). This is a high dependency ratio and is characteristic of developing countries around the world. There is high percentage (more than 35%) of population in the age group 0-14 years, which can be considered beneficial as this young generation will add to the working population of India in coming decades. The Census of India, 2011 published a special series on the population of children of age 0-6 years. Most of the southern states of Maharashtra, Karnataka, Tamil Nadu & Andhra Pradesh and West Bengal, Delhi, Himachal Pradesh & Punjab have less than 12% of its population who are children (0-6 years old). Whereas in Jammu and Kashmir, Rajasthan, Uttar Pradesh, Jharkhand, Meghalaya and Arunachal Pradesh more than 15% of population is composed of 0-6 age group children.

Table 1.6 Broad Age Groups of Population (% of total population)

Year	0-14 years	15-59 years	60 and above
1901	38.1	56.8	5.1
1911	37.8	56.9	5.2
1921	38.6	56.0	5.4
1931	38.5	56.4	5.1
1941	39.1	55.2	5.7
1951	37.5	56.9	5.6
1961	41.0	53.3	5.6
1971	42.0	52.0	6.0
1981	39.7	54.1	6.2
1991	37.8	55.5	6.7

Source: Census of India, 2001

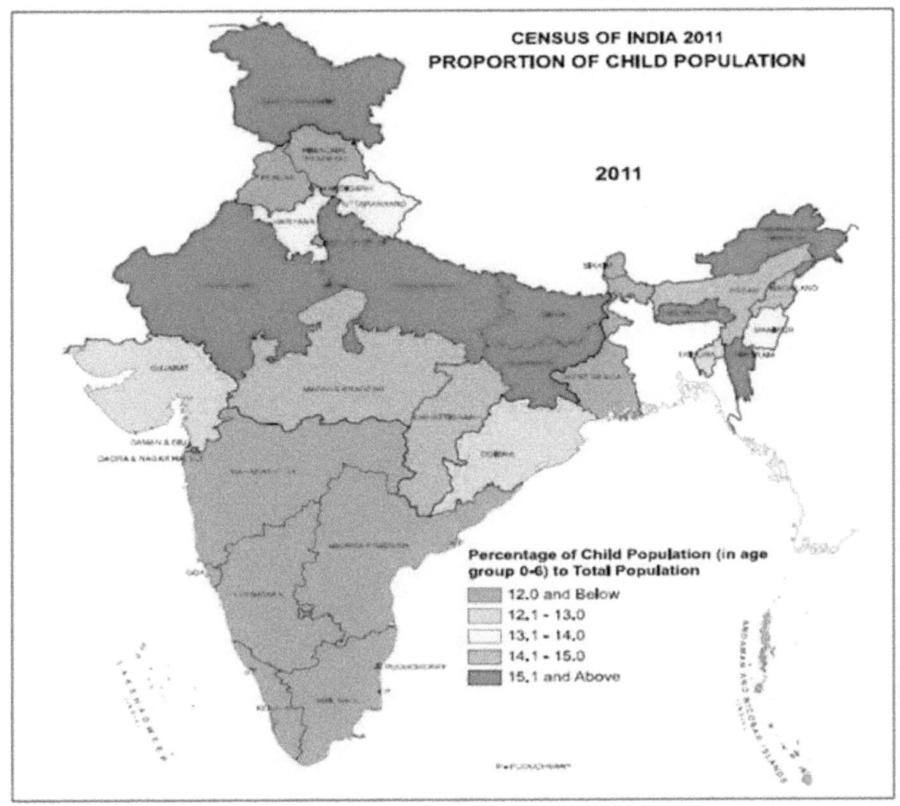

Fig. 1.6: Percentage of child population between 0-6 years of age. *Source: Census of India*

SEX RATIO

Sex ratio can be defined as the number of females per 1000 males. The sex ratio trends in India from 1901 to 2011 are given in Table 1.7. In majority of the time, the trend shows a declining sex ratio (except in 1951, 1981, 2001 and 2011). The preference for male child in India is primarily due to its strong patriarchal nature. This bias against girl child and parental determination of sex has been detrimental for the females in the country. Female infanticides along with the high mortality rate of mothers during child birth have resulted in a reduction in the sex ratio. In 1901 there were 972 females per 1000 males, however, according to the 2011 census, now there are 940 females per 1000 males. Though there has been a decreasing trend in the sex ratios, the sex ratio has been growing since the past three decades. In 1991, the sex ratios were 927 and in 2001 it was 933. Since then it has grown to 940 in 2011.

The table below shows the sex ratio by state from Census 2011. The states with low (<900) sex ratios are Jammu and Kashmir, Punjab, Haryana, Delhi, Sikkim and Andaman & Nicobar Islands. The states with high sex ratios (>976) are Kerala, Tamil Nadu, Pondicherry, Odisha, Chhattisgarh, Meghalaya, Manipur, Mizoram and Arunachal Pradesh.

Year	No. of Females per 1000 males
1901	972
1911	964
1921	955
1931	950
1941	945
1951	946
1961	941
1971	930
1981	934
1991	927
2001	933
2011	940

Table 1.7 Trends in sex ratio in India.*Source: Census of India, 2011*

LITERACY

The working definition of literacy in the Indian census since 1991 is the total percentage of the population of an area at a particular time aged seven years or above who can read and write with understanding. It is an index of quality of human life and human development. It is representative of economic development, standard of living, status of women and technological advances. Literacy in India in 1901 was merely 5.35%, but has reached to 74.04% in 2011. Still, India has the largest illiterate population in the world, and this poses to be a stumbling block in the development of the country. Though literacy in women has also grown 11 times than it was in 1901 (only 0.60%), it still stagers behind the male literate population.

At state level, Kerala with 93.91% literacy in 2011 has the highest literacy in India, whereas Bihar has the lowest literacy of 63.82%. Table 6.10 shows state-wise literacy in India.

OCCUPATION STRUCTURE

The rate of growth in workforce is 1.8% between 2001 and 2011 and though it is observed to be marginally higher than that of the population growth rate; this rate is lower than that of previous two decades (1980s and 1990s). However, the rate of growth in workforce has always been higher than that of population growth during the last three decades, suggesting an increase in work participation rate.

Nearly 67% of the working population in primary sector (agriculture and similar activities) and only 12% in secondary and 13% tertiary sector. There has been a small decline in the primary workforce from 1911 to 1991 (7.8%). This is indicative of slow economic growth, a heavy dependence on agriculture and insufficient employment opportunities in secondary sector.

A significant characteristic of the Indian occupation structure is the low participation of females in the working population of India. Females contribute to only about 22.5% in the country's total working population and majority of them are in agriculture. Furthermore, more female workers work as marginal employees than male workers. Census classifies workers into two categories— main and marginal workers. The main workers work for more than six months in a year and the marginal workers work for less than six months. Therefore, more females work in temporary or short term jobs. While 55.5% of the population is in the working age group (15- 59 age group), only about 34% of the population is counted towards a working population, showing that a significant amount of the country's manpower is not utilized.

SUMMARY

The population of India is diverse and contributes to 17% of the total world population. As of 2011, only 74.04 % of the population is literate and 34% is in the work force. Though there has been a tremendous increase in literacy and occupation, the country still hosts the largest population of the illiterates in the world. The sex ratio of India is 940 and though there has been a decreasing trend in the sex ratios, it has been growing since the past three decades, which is a positive sign. However, biases against women in the country continue to hinder their development, which is also evident in the occupation structure: most females work as marginal workers and number of female workers is significantly less than the male workers. Urbanization continues to pull population into better-developed areas, thereby increasing population density in those areas. The hilly states with less favorable conditions for human inhabitance continue causes migration of population into areas with more opportunities and a better quality life.

GLOSSARY

- **Age structure** is the proportion of a population in different age groups. Age structure is one of the most important factors in determining the proportion working population available that can contribute to the labor force and the dependent population in the total population.
- **Demographic Divide:** The year of 1921 is acknowledged as the "Demographic Divide" between the period of stagnant or fluctuating growth and the period marked by steady population growth. The year 1951 marked yet another "Demographic Divide" in the growth history of India's population. At this stage, a tremendous amount of increase was witnessed: the country's population increased by approximately 284% between 1951- 2011.
- **Literacy:** The working definition of literacy in the Indian census since 1991 is the total percentage of the population of an area at a particular time aged seven years or above who can read and write with understanding. It is an index of quality of human life and human development. It is representative of economic development, standard of living, status of women and technological advances.
- **Main and Marginal workers:** Census classifies workers into two categories— main and marginal workers. The main workers work for more than six months in a year and the marginal workers work for less than six months.
- **Migration** is the movement of people from one place to another temporarily of permanently and is composed of four types: rural to rural, rural to urban, urban to rural and urban to urban. Migration to and from any area primarily influences the distribution of the population in the

region. The main cause of migration is economic factors, but factors like marriage, social insecurity, political disturbances, and inter-ethnic conflicts also contribute to migrations.

- **Population density** is the measure of persons inhabiting a unit area of land. For example, the population density of India in 2011 was calculated to be 382 persons per square km.
- **Resource Regions** are the regions that have big industrial ad urban clusters with significant scientific and technological resource potential to attract more population. For examples, resource region such as the West Bengal Deltaic Region has a significant pulling affect over the rural population.
- **Sex ratio** can be defined as the number of females per 1000 males.
- **Stagnant population phase,** continued from the 1800's into early 1900's. the population from 1901-1921 witnessed a stagnant population, increasing from about 238 million in 1901 to about 251 million 1921, resulting in an average growth rate of 0.27% per annum.
- **Urbanization** is the migration of population from not very well developed rural areas such as villages to well-developed urban areas such as cities. This gradual or rapid increase in the proportion of people living in urban areas, cause cities to grow physically as well.

CHECK YOUR PROGRESS:

1. Population distribution refers to how people are spread across a geographical area.
2. Population density is the number of people living in a given area, usually expressed per square kilometer or square mile.
3. Population growth can be influenced by factors such as birth rates, death rates, immigration, and emigration.
4. The sex ratio is a measure of the balance between males and females in a population.
5. In many countries, there is a slightly higher proportion of females compared to males.
6. Literacy rates measure the percentage of people in a population who can read and write at a basic level.

7. High literacy rates are often associated with better economic and social development.
8. Population composition can refer to various demographic factors such as age, ethnicity, and religion.
9. Aging populations have a higher proportion of elderly individuals, which can impact healthcare and social services.
10. Urban areas tend to have higher population densities compared to rural areas.
11. Some countries have negative population growth due to low birth rates and emigration.
12. Developing countries often experience faster population growth compared to developed nations.
13. In many regions, efforts are made to improve female literacy and reduce gender disparities.
14. Population data is essential for governments and policymakers to plan for services and infrastructure.

REFERENCES

1. Census of India: 1961,1971,1981,1991,2001,2011

1. Registrar General, 2001: Census of India, 2001, India, 2A, Mansingh Road, New Delhi110011, 25th July, 2001
2. Gautam, (2015) "Advanced Geography of India", Fourth Revised Edition, Allahabad.
3. Despande, S.andDespande, L. (1998) " Impact of Liberalisation of Labour Market in India: What Do Facts from NSSO's 50th Round Show" Economic and Political Weekly, Vol.33No 22, pp L21-L31
4. Singh, R.L. (1973); Urban Geography in Developing Countries. NGSI: Varanasi
5. Kundu, A (1983): "Theories of City Size Distribution and Indian Urban Structure – A Reappraisal", Economic and Political weekly, 18(3).
6. Mishra, R.P. and K. Mishra (1988); Million Cities in India. New Delhi
7. M. Venkatanarayana and Suresh V. Naik, Growth and Structure of Workforce in India : An Analysis of Census 2011 Data

TERMINAL QUESTIONS

A- LONG QUESTIONS

1. Write about the Literacy profile of India taking into account the male and female populations.
2. Describe the factors involved in the distribution of Population.
3. What are the major "pull" and "push" factors that are responsible for migration?
4. What trends are present in the growth of population from 1901 to 2011? Why was there a "stagnant" phase?
5. Comment on the urbanization in India and how has it influenced the population distribution?
6. What is the occupation structure of India? What does the latest data show regarding male and female participation in the working force of India?
7. Which are the most populous and the least populous states?
8. Why is the year 1921 referred to as the "Demographic Divide"?
9. What are resource regions? Why do they attract more population?
10. What was the stagnant population phase in the population growth history of India?
11. Which age group is considered the "working force" and which is considered "dependable"?
12. What is urbanization?
13. What is migration? What is meant by "push" and "pull" factors?
14. Which states have the highest and the lowest sex ratio?
15. Which state has the highest literacy and how much?
16. What is the difference between "main" and "marginal" worker?

B- SHORT QUESTIONS

1. Define the term population distribution. How the population of India is distributed?
2. What is population density? Present an overview of India's population density.
3. Describe the population growth of India.
4. What is Urbanization? How India's population is urbanizing?

5. Why India's average sex ratio is decreasing? Explain
6. Explain the literacy rate of India as per 2011 census.
7. What is main reason behind the faster population growth in India?

C- MULTIPLE CHOICE QUESTIONS

1. Which age group constitutes the largest portion of India's population?

A. 0-14 years

B. 15-24 years

C. 25-54 years

D. 55+ years

Answer: (A) 0-14 years

2. Which state in India has the highest female literacy rate?

A. Kerala

B. Bihar

C. Uttar Pradesh

D. Rajasthan

Answer: (A) Kerala

3. What is the term used to describe the movement of people from rural areas to urban areas?

A. Urbanization

B. Migration

C. Industrialization

D. Ruralization

Answer: b) Migration

4. Which city is often referred to as the "Financial Capital of India" and has a significant population?

A. Mumbai

B. Delhi

C. Bangalore

D. Chennai

Answer: (A) Mumbai

5. What is the main reason for the high population growth rate in India?

A. Increased life expectancy

B. Improved healthcare

C. High birth rate

D. Declining fertility rate Answer: (C) High birth rate

6. Which state has the highest population growth rate among the major Indian states?

A. Bihar

B. Uttar Pradesh

C. Madhya Pradesh

D. Rajasthan

Answer: (A) Bihar

7. What is the name of the government program initiated to control India's population Growth through family planning and reproductive health services?

A. Swachh Bharat Abhiyan

B. Make in India

C. Beti Bachao, Beti Padhao

D. Family Planning Program Answer: (D) Family Planning Program

8. State with highest population density is

A. Uttar Pradesh

B. Bihar

C. West Bengal

D. Haryana

Answer: (B) Bihar

9. As per census of 2011, what is the density of India?

A. 302

B. 402

C. 382

D. 482

Answer: (C) 382

10. During which decade the populations record a negative growth rate?

A. 1921-1931

B. 1911- 1921

C. 1931- 1941

D. 1941- 1951

Answer: (B) 1911-1921

CHAPTER TWO

URBANIZATION

INTRODUCTION

Urbanization is no longer a phenomenon peculiar only to certain parts of the world rather it is a worldwide phenomenon. According to 2001 census, the urban population of India was 286.11 million, living in 5161 towns, which constitutes 27.81% of the total country's population. However, the same as per 2011 census has risen to 377.16 million viz. 32.16% of the total country's population and at the same time number of towns has gone up to 7935. The rate of urban growth in the country is very high as compared to developed countries, and the large cities are becoming larger mostly due to continuous migration of population to these cities. India's current urban population exceeds the whole population of the United States, the world's third largest country. By 2050, over half of India's population is expected to be urban dwellers. This creates enormous pressure on existing urban infrastructure. Over the years, there has been continuous concentration of population in class I towns. On the contrary the concentration of population in medium and small towns either fluctuated or declined. The graduation of number of urban centers from lower population size categories to class I cities has resulted top heavy structure of urban population in India indicating the tendency towards concentration in larger agglomerations. Urban accumulation is a continuous urban spread constituting a town and its adjoining urban out growths (OGs) or two or more physical contiguous town together and any adjoining urban out growths of such towns. Examples of out growths are railway colonies, university campus, port area, military campus, etc. that may come up near a statutory town or city. Therefore India's urbanization is often termed as over- urbanization and or pseudo-urbanization. The large population size is leading to virtual collapse in the urban services and followed by basic problems in the field of housing, slum, water, infrastructure, quality of life, etc.

URBANIZATION AND ITS TRENDS

It explains the chief form of the condition of life. It represents a revolutionary change in the whole pattern of social life. A number of scholars forwarded their views on this issue. Queen and Carpenter have said that, "the word urban is used to identify the phenomena of city". Wirth says, that 'urbanism denotes the way of life'.

Urbanization is important event of modern times. The high growth in population of town and high increase in the number of towns are the main features of the modern period. According to G. T. Trewartha, the level of urbanization is defined as the proportion of total population, residing in urban places. However, the rate of urbanization is the percent increase over a given period of time in the proportion of total population living in urban communities.

According to E.E. Bergel, "the conversion of village into urban areas is known as the process of urbanization".

Fig. 2.1: Urbanization in Indian Cities.

It is apparent from the above definitions that urbanization is not static, but it is dynamic. The speed of urbanization is affected by the economy of an area. This economy speed up towards agricultural economy, it is also accelerates the urbanization. The increase in the population of towns takes place and also there are continuous increases in their number and also at the same time the ratios of urban population also increase in total population.

CYCLE OF URBANIZATION

G. T. Trewartha says that urbanization is a cyclical process through with nations pass as they evolve from agrarian to industrial societies. Urban process denotes the increase in ratio or urban population to total population. This increase, if it begins, then it also becomes still at certain point. In developed nation of the world, the urbanization took rapid speed in the first hundreds years. Some nations noted fall in this ratio. Thus, the urbanization curve has the shape of an attenuated 'S'. Different nations and regions reach at different points on the curve at different times.

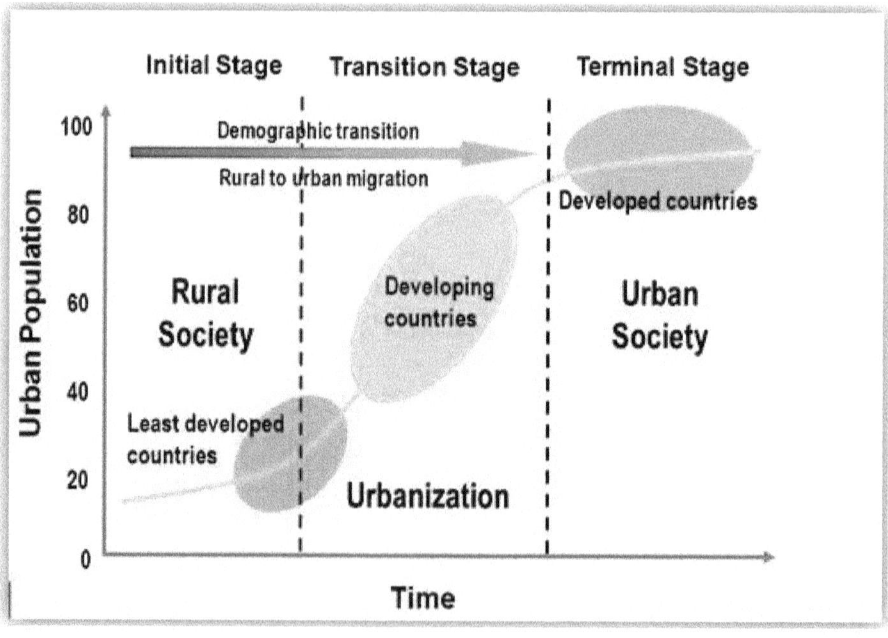

Fig.2.2: Cycle of Urbanization with Different Stages.

I. <u>First stage of urbanization (initial stage):</u>The flattish, lower end of the curve depicts the conditions of an early time period, and is called initial stage of urbanization. It has the slow rise in the ratio of urban population to total population. This ratio is found up to 25%. This line has low steepness. It is characterized by an economic structure known as the traditional society. The emphasis here is on agrarian sector of the economy, which has characteristically been accompanied by a dispersed population, a relatively small share of which resides in cities. In this initial stage of urbanization, the following nations can be put into this group- Uganda, Tanzania, Sudan, Ethiopia, Kenya, Mauritania, Zambia, Madagascar, Nepal, Bangladesh, Indonesia, Thailand, Malaysia, Pakistan etc.

II. <u>Second Stage of Urbanization (Acceleration Stage):</u>The reduced trunk of the urbanization curve is referred to as the acceleration. This stage shows the steepness of urbanization. The curve line is just like a vertical line. The steepness goes up to 75% population being urban. During this stage, there is a concentration not only on people but of economic activities as well. Manufacturing industries, trade and services employ increasingly large number of people and become more significant. On the other hand the opportunity of employment declines in the primary sector that includes agriculture. A number of nations of Europe, Asia, South America and South-west Asia have reached in the acceleration stage of urbanization.

III. <u>Third Stage of Urbanization (Terminal Stage):</u>This stage denotes the beginning of the share of urban population 75 percent or more. Hence, the curve line finishes its steepness. Sometimes, this line shows a bend; otherwise it is a flattish urban curve. England in 1861, Belgium in 1910 and Sweden in 1920 have attained the position of flattish urban curve. Here the rate of urbanization becomes very slow. The urbanization has reached up to its last limit in Sweden, Belgium, Israel, Australia and New Zealand. More than 80 percent populations of these nations live in cities.

URBANIZATION IN INDIA

The study of urbanization in India by its very nature involves several dimension of analysis. Fundamentally, urbanization is a socio-economic process by which an increasing proportion of an area becomes concentrated in urban areas. India is the most populous country in the world after China. India's fast growing urbanization has a regional as well as world-wide impact. India's urban population constitutes a sizeable proportion of the world's urban population. This can be well corroborated from the fact that every 12th city dweller of the world and every 7th of the developing countries is the Indian. India has as many small towns (population 100,000 - 499,999) as in the United States; and as many metropolises (population +500,000) as in Australia, France and Brazil combined.

Urbanization in India can be studied through Census data provided at a regular interval of 10 years since 1881 onwards. These data help us in analyzing the trends of growth in the urban population, decennial increase, urbanization and number of towns during the 20th century.

The growth of urbanization in India is basically through two ways, one is through increase in the urban population, which is natural and the second one is through migration, which is result of people migrating from rural to urban areas and also from small towns/cities to big metros. However, in 1990s, i.e. when the Indian government opened up their economy, there seen a rise in rapid economic growth of the country. But this economic growth was more of urban growth, which led to rapid migration of rural population to urban areas.

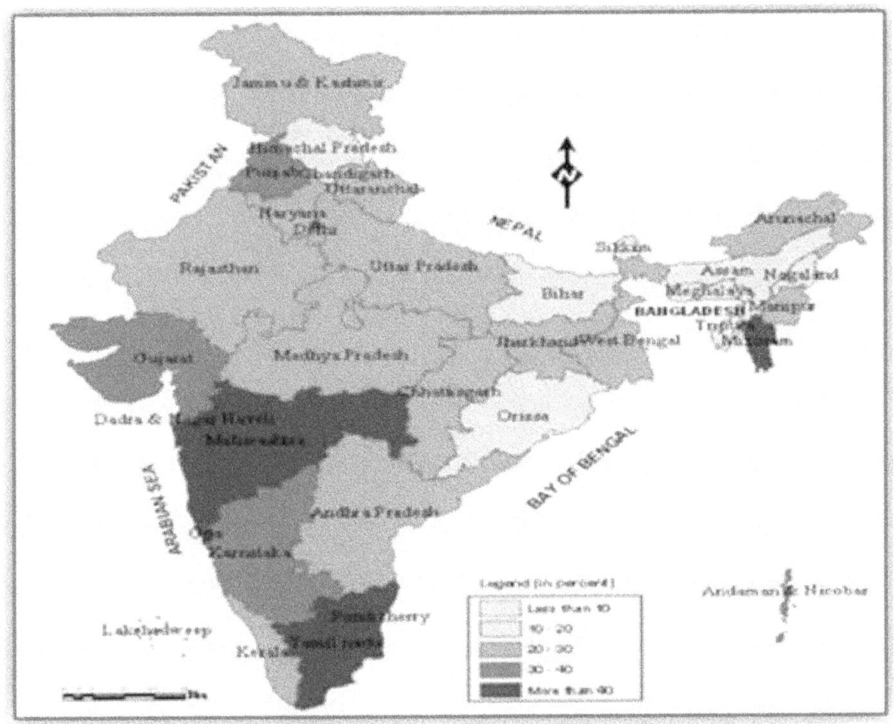

Fig.2.3: Spatial Pattern of Urbanization in India.

In the year 1951, only five cities were having population of more than one million, which increased to 53 cities in 2011 and it was estimated that by 2031, it will be to 70 cities in the country with million populations. Similarly, three cities are having more than 10 million populations in the year 2011, and it was estimated that six cities will be having 10 million populations by 2031. Thus, it was estimated that the total urban population by the year 2030 will be 610 million, which will account for the 40% of the total population of the country (Mohan, 2012). The many cities in our country, are becoming extremely crowded and if we see the 20 most densely populated cities in the world, out of which five will be from India including, Kolkata and Mumbai (Confederation of Indian Industry, 2010).

As per the World Urbanization Prospects: 2011 Revision, the percentage of total urban population in India is 30.9 in 2010, which is lower than the developed countries like the United States of America (82.1 per cent) and

Japan (90.5 percent) during the same year. It is also lower than in other fast growing developing countries, such as, China (49.2 per cent), Brazil (84.3), and Russian Federation (73.7 per cent) in 2010. India's urban population is mainly concentrated in and around class I cities. The percentage share of urban population in class I cities has increased from 51.42 in 1961 to 68.7 in 2001. On the other hand, classes II to VI cities have registered a decreasing rate of urban population growth (percentage). For instance, the percentage share of urban population in class IV cities decreased from 12.77 in 1961 to 6.84 in 2001.

PHASES OF URBANIZATION IN INDIA

According to Census of India, 2001, nearly 286.12 million people in country live in urban places constituting about 27.8 percent of total population. On the basis of trends of urbanization in India during the 20th century, following three distinct phases may be identified.

1. Period of Slow Urbanization (1901-31): In the beginning of twentieth century (1901), the urban population of India was 25.85 million forming 1084 percent of total population. The growth rate of urban population during first and second decades was amazingly low being only 0.35 percent and 8.27 percent respectively. The growth has been steady till 1931 but after that the urban population showed an explosive growth. The decadal growth rate in India's urban population in third decades was recorded as 19.21 percent. In 1931, about 3346 million people forming 11.99 percent of total population of the country lived in 2049 urban places.

Year	Number of Towns	Total urban population (million)	Decadal Variation (percent)	Percentage of urban to total population
1901	1834	25.85	-	10.84
1911	1776	25.94	0.35	10.29
1921	1921	28.09	8.27	11.71
1931	2049	33.46	19.12	11.99
1941	2210	44.13	31.97	13.86
1951	2844	62.44	41.43	17.29
1961	2330	78.94	26.61	17.97
1971	2531	109.11	38.23	19.91
1981	3245	159.46	46.61	23.13
1991	3609	217.61	36.47	26.13
2001	3799	286.12	31.48	27.81
2011	4041	377.11	31.80	31.16

Table 2.1: Growth of Urbanization in India since 1901 *Source: Census of India, 1991 to 2011*

2. **Period of Medium Urbanization (1931-61):** The period between 1931 and 1961 may be considered as a period of medium urbanization in India. The year shows a significant demographic divide in the history of urban growth in the county. In 1931 urban population of the country was 33.46 million which rose to 44.15 million in 1941, 62.44 million in 1951 and 78.94 million in 1961. Thus, the percentage of urban to total population rose from 11.99 percent in 1931 to 17.97 percent in 1961. The decadal variation was recorded as 31.97, 41.43 and 26.41 during fourth, fifth and sixth decades respectively. The number of towns which was 2049 in 1931 became 2330 in 1961. It is noteworthy that a number of small towns were de-classified from the list of towns in 1961 census because of more strict definition of town adopted by Census of India.

3. **Period of Rapid Urbanization (1961-1991):** The urban development in India got momentum after 1961 due to the stabilization of the economic development and industrialization growth. Consequently, the urban population of the country increased from 78.94 million in 1961 to 286.12

million in 2001, showing a growth of 262.0 percent during 40 years. The percentage of urban population to total population which was 17.97 percent reached 23.31 percent in 1981 and 27.81 percent in 2001. Similarly, number of towns and cities rose from 2330 in 1961 to 4041 in 2011. It is marked that, here the urban agglomeration is treated as one unit otherwise number of towns comes to be 7935.

4. Period of High Rapid Urbanization (1991-till now): During these decades, 159.9 million urban populations were added. This addition is just equivalent to the urban population of 1981. The percentage of urban population was increased from 25.72 to 31.61 percent. This period noted as an addition of 4326 new towns. It is clear that a number of villages are proceeding towards urbanization. It is also observed that metropolitan cities are making impressive increase in their population size. These were 23 in number in 1991, but this number touched the figure of 53 in 2011.

SPATIAL PATTERN OF LEVEL OF URBANIZATION

I. <u>**Urban Population Ratio:**</u>People living in towns and urban agglomerations with a population of 20,000 or more accounted for 20.5 percent of India's total population of 683 million in 1981. In relation to developed countries this represents a low level of urbanization. While no country in the world has the whole of its population in towns of 20,000 or more, a number of countries have over 60 per cent of their population living in such places. The percentage of population living in urban centers in India is increasing at an annual rate of approximately 2 percent. In 1971, the percentage of population in 20,000-plus towns was 16.1 and there was a 25 per cent increase during the decade 1971-81. While the percentage will continue to increase in the future, it may not reach the level prevalent in developed countries for decades to come.

There are significant variations in the level of urbanization (as measured by the percentage of urban population) between the different states in India. Maharashtra and Tamil Nadu have more than 30 per cent of their population living in towns; they are the most urbanized states in India. Gujarat and West Bengal also have a very high level of urbanization with just over 25 per cent of their population in towns. The least urbanized state is Arunachal Pradesh, which has no towns with a population of 20,000 or more. This state and the union territories of Lakshadweep and Dadra and Nagar Haveli are the least urbanized areas of the country. In Himachal Pradesh only 2.6 per cent of the population lives in towns of 20,000 or more. Urbanization is at a lower level in the north-eastern region, including Assam, Nagaland, Tripura and Manipur; and in the area of the Ganga plains covering Uttar Pradesh and Bihar. Orissa has the lowest level of urbanization, 9 percent, among the bigger states in India. In general terms western and southern India is relatively highly urbanized while eastern and northern India are least urbanized.

The least urbanized states have the following characteristics: (a) they are hilly or mountainous, (b) they have a larger proportion of tribal population, and (c) they are generally in accessible with respect to metropolitan cities and the main arterial railways connecting them. But the plains of Orissa and Bihar, where the three characteristics noted above are absent, stand out as unexplained pockets of low levels of urbanization.

II. **Structural Patterns:** A important aspect of urbanization all over the world is the uneven pattern of development of small towns and big cities within the system. Every urban system is characterized by the presence of a few large cities and a large number of small towns. The large cities account for a larger share of the total urban population, while the small towns, despite their numbers, account for a smaller share. This is true of the Indian urban system, and is brought out in table.

The million cities form the apex of the Indian urban system and account for over a quarter of India's urban population. They are followed closely by the one-lakh cities and the medium towns, each of which accounts for over a quarter of the urban population. Together these three categories add up to more than 85 per cent of the urban population. The small towns, which account for 55 per cent of the total number of towns, constitute only 13 per cent of the urban population. The mini towns have a trivial role in India's urban system. The distribution patterns of the major categories of cities and towns in the different states of India show remarkable unevenness.

III. **The Metropolis and the City:** Figure below illustrates that, according to 2001 census, the net addition was 546 new towns i.e., an increase of 11.83 percent during 1991-2001. The highest increase is evident in class III towns, where the number of towns increased from 517 to 1387 during 1961-2001. The number of cities (or class I towns) has risen from 105 in 1961 to 441 in 2001. The number of towns in class I to class V has been steadily rising since 1961. The total number of metropolitan cities (population one million and above) in India has increased from 23 in 1991 to 35 in 2001 and on to 53 by 2011. In addition, the number of towns has increased from 2657 in 1961 to 7935 in 2011. The results indicate an increasing trend in the addition of new cities/ towns in India.

Of the 28 states in India, 17 have no million cities. None of the union territories, excepting Delhi, possesses a million cities. While the smaller states and the union territories cannot be expected to have million cities, there are large states, in particular Bihar and Madhya Pradesh, which have no million cities. Both states ought to have these, considering the size of their population. However, they fall within the urban shadow of two leading metropolitan cities of India, namely Kolkata and Delhi. The four principal metropolitan cities account for the absence of million cities in a number of peripheral states and union territories. Thus, the state of Kerala comes under the shadow of Chennai; Jammu and Kashmir, Punjab, Himachal Pradesh and Haryana come under the influence of Delhi, while Bihar, Orissa and the entire northeastern area come under the shadow of Kolkata.

A number of states, however, have fully developed and independent urban systems with their own million cities at the apex. There were 8 such large states in India in 1981. Maharashtra had three cities with populations of a million or more, while Uttar Pradesh had two such cities in close proximity to each other. However, a major part of Uttar Pradesh comes directly under the influence of Delhi, the national capital. The other states where the urban system is dominated by one metropolitan city are the three southern states of Tamil Nadu, Karnataka and Andhra Pradesh, and the states of Gujarat, West Bengal and Rajasthan.

At a lower level, the one-lakh cities play an important role in the Indian urban system. There were over 200 such cities in India in 1981. In spite of this, the entire states of Goa, Himachal Pradesh, Mizoram, Nagaland and Sikkim, and all Union Territories, excepting Delhi, Chandigarh and Pondicherry, had not even a single one-lakh city. In fact, all these territorial units are small in terms of their total population 'which is less than 5 million in each case.

Several other states had urban systems with one city at the apex; they include Meghalaya, Manipur and Assam (1971). Each of the larger states, with a population of 10 million or more, had several one-lakh cities. Among these states, Haryana, Kerala, Bihar, West Bengal, Andhra Pradesh, Maharashtra and Tamil Nadu had a relatively higher proportion of one-lakh cities. One- lakh cities were deficient in Punjab, Uttar Pradesh, Rajasthan, Madhya Pradesh and Gujarat. This points to minor structural deficiencies in the urban systems of these states.

Medium Towns: The medium towns form an important link function within an urban system. They can serve to offset the deficiencies in the number of larger cities as well as of small towns. Medium towns account for over a quarter of the total number of towns as well as the total urban population. In terms of numbers, the medium towns are very strongly represented in the states of Kerala, Maharashtra and Andhra Pradesh, where they account for Over 50 per cent of the total number of towns. In West Bengal, Tamil Nadu and Bihar, they account for slightly over 40 per cent. The medium towns are poorly developed in Uttar Pradesh, Assar, Madhya Pradesh among the larger states, and Himachal Pradesh, Manipur, Meghalaya, Sikkim and Tripura among the smaller states. Medium towns form the largest urban centers in the states of Himachal Pradesh, Sikkim and Nagaland where they are called upon to act as the state capitals: Shimla, Gangtok and Kohima. These towns often do not have the infrastructure required to perform such a function. In the case of Shimla, this is offset by the fact that it was the summer capital of British India, but Gangtok and Kohima are less well off. In all three cases, however, the constraints of hilly location and cold winters inhibit further expansion. Elsewhere, medium towns are major market centers for agricultural produce and have a rural oriented tertiary sector. Few of these towns have any appreciable industrial base.

Small Towns and Mini Towns: The smaller states and union territories as well as the less urbanized among the larger states, have a larger proportion of small towns. In these cases, the small towns constitute more than 60 per cent of the total number of towns. Among the big states, Madhya Pradesh, Uttar Pradesh, Orissa, Rajasthan and Assam are notable for the high proportion of small towns. Kerala has a lower proportion of small towns. The mini towns, though not large in number, are an important component of the urban systems of Sikkim, Meghalaya, Manipur, Himachal Pradesh, Jammu and Kashmir, and Tripura. Among the largest states, Uttar Pradesh has as many as 82 mini towns: more than a third of the 230 mini towns in the country. Mini towns are a characteristic feature of the hill areas, particularly in Himachal Pradesh, Manipur and Jammu and Kashmir.

In these areas, the nature of the terrain accounts for the small size of both rural and urban settlements. Most of the mini towns of Uttar Pradesh also belong to the hill tracts of Kumaon and Gharwal districts. Those in the plains are actually project towns, collieries, or small industrial townships. By and large, most mini towns have clear and specific urban attributes.

The identification of small towns, on the other hand, poses a problem. Small towns have a population of 5,000 or more; however, the number of revenue villages with a population of 5,000 or more is roughly 10,800, and of these only 1,790 are recognized by the Census as small towns. The inter-state differences in the number and ratio of small towns are least in part, due to the Census definition of urban areas.

REGIONAL PATTERN OF URBANIZATION

India's 3.77.11 million people forming 31.16 percent of its total population live in 4041 urban places but the distribution of towns and urban population even level of urbanization is not even in the states and union territories of the country. Table below illustrates that some states have higher level of urbanization while some other have very low and are in its initial stage. On the basis of level of urbanization all the states and union territories are classified into following three groups:

1. **Highly Urbanized Region (50 percent and above):** Three small political units- Delhi (97.50 percent), Chandigarh (97.25 percent), and Puducherry (68.31 percent) are highly urbanized where more than 65 percent population resides in urban centers. Due to small area and high concentration of urban population, the urban density in Delhi and Chandigarh is above 7000 persons per square kilometers. Puducherry also have urban density above 1400 persons per square kilometers. Delhi is the national capital while Chandigarh is the capital of Punjab, Haryana and Chandigarh, Lakshadweep, Daman and Diu, Goa and Mizoram are also small regions and highly urbanized.

2. **Medium Urbanized Region (25-50 percent):** This category of urbanization includes states and union territories of the country where level of urbanization ranges 25 to 50 percent. The states and union territories of this group are Tamil Nadu, Kerala, Maharashtra, Gujarat, Karnataka, Punjab, Andaman and Nicobar island, Haryana, West Bengal,

Andhra Pradesh, Manipur, Madhya Pradesh, Uttarakhand, Nagaland, Jammu and Kashmir and Tripura.

3. **Less Urbanized Region (Less than 25 percent):** 11 states and union territories are included in this category. In this category Sikkim stands on highest position followed by Rajasthan and Jharkhand. In Uttar Pradesh, Arunachal Pradesh, Chhattisgarh and Meghalaya about 20.0 percent population lives in urban centers. Other states such as Orissa, Assam, Bihar and Himachal Pradesh have very low percentage of urban population (below 20 percent). Himachal Pradesh (10.4 percent) is the least urbanized state followed by Bihar (11.10 percent) and Assam (14.08 percent).

MAIN CHARACTERSTICS OF INDIAN URBANIZATION

1. India has a long history of urbanization which began as early as in 3000 B.C. when a number of urban centers flourished in Indus valley.
2. The process of urbanization in India was very slow till beginning of the 20th century. The growth rate of urban population during first and second decades was amazingly low to the effect of famine and influenza epidemic. The urban population showed an explosive growth after 1931. The period of rapid urbanization started since 6th decade of twentieth century.
3. The urbanization in the past was largely possible by means of rural-urban migration and this feature is still highly significant in the process of urbanization in India. The rural push created by rural population pressure, poverty and unemployment is a major factor in the growth of cities in India.
4. Studying urbanization in India, Peach observed: Industrialization and urbanization, so stably married in the industrialization are often divorced in India. The match-makers of policy aimed at industrialization. Here the rate of industrialization, however, has failed to keep pace with urbanization which has created a number of socio-economic problems there.
5. The process of urbanization in India is of subsistence nature. Here uneducated even illiterate and unskilled people from rural areas swarm into large towns and cities to seek employment. Most of them remain either unemployed or are low paid. Consequently they may be eating

worse food and live in worse house of slums. This urban ward migration affects badly the quality of city life in India.

6. In India, urban centers particularly large town and cities are growing more on the basis of tertiary sector rather than on the basis of secondary sectors.

7. The level of urbanization is higher in southern India than in northern India, and western part is more urbanized then eastern part of the country.

THE PROBLEMS OF URBANIZATION

The use of modern technology is increased in cities in the industrial fields. So the figure of employees is increasing more rather than the figure of employment. Hence, urban unemployment increases. It is due to urbanization, the problem of habitat emerges. So people live in filthy Chaws, roads which give birth to theft, loot, prostitution etc...The pollution of air, water and noise increases in cities due to industrial development and increasing vehicles.

1. **Rural urban migration:** A large part of migration and urbanization in India have been linked to stagnation and volatility of agriculture and lack of sectorial diversification within agrarian economy. The growth rates in agricultural production and income has been noted to be low, unstable and disparate across regions over the past several decades, resulting in lack of livelihood opportunities in rural areas. A low rate of infrastructural investment in public sector in the period of structural adjustment - necessary for keeping budgetary deficits low - also have affected agriculture adversely. This has led to out-migration from several backward rural areas, most of the migrants being absorbed within urban informal economy. But the capacity of the cities and towns to assimilate the migrants by providing employment, access to land, basic amenities etc. are limited. The problem have acquired severity as migrants have shown high selectivity in choosing their destinations (understandably linked with availability of employment and other opportunities), leading to regionally unbalanced urbanization as also distortions in urban hierarchy. Rural urban migration has often been considered the major factor for growth of slums in urban areas.

2. **Emergence of slums:** The most important problem in all cities has been housing the sudden and large scale influx of migrants from rural areas to urban areas especially the metropolises and state capitals. Due to lack of housing, in every city almost fifty percent population lives in slums. Slums known as bustees (Basties) in India, favelas in Brazil, katchiabadis in Pakistan and focus insalubres in Cuba, all have few characteristics in common:

- Poor structural quality and durability of housing.
- Insufficient living areas (more than three people sharing a room).
- Lack of secure tenure.
- Poor access to water.

3. **Urban transport:** India is transiting from a developing to developed country with high pace of economic development. Urbanization is too increasing at high pace as mega cities, cities and towns are providing better economic opportunities. Fast growing cities have nurtured business and industry, and have provided jobs and higher incomes to many migrants from rural areas. Thus, it is important that cities function efficiently, that their resources are used to maximize the cities' contribution to national income. City efficiency largely depends upon the effectiveness of its transport systems, i.e., efficacy with which people and goods are moved throughout the city. Poor transport systems hampers economic growth and development, and the net effect may be a loss of competitiveness in both domestic as well as international markets.

4. **Waste disposable:** Removing garbage, cleaning drains and unclogging sewers are the main jobs of municipalities and municipal corporations in Indian cities. In most cities, the municipal service for the collection and transportation of urban solid wastes comprises three separate functions as follows:

- Sweeping, curbside and domestic waste collection from garbage bins.
- Transportation by handcarts to large or road collection points, which may be open dumps.
- Transportation by vehicles to the disposal sites.

The weaknesses of the existing system of solid waste management are:

i. the professional and managerial capacities of the municipal bodies are limited and this is more pronounced in case of smaller cities;
ii. no charges are levied for garbage collection or disposal, nor are there any incentives for reducing garbage or recycling waste;
iii. no separate costing is done for this function;
iv. indiscriminate use of plastic bags and goods;
v. recourse to modern technology is rare and;
vi. segregation of garbage at the source is not enforced.

5. **Water drainage and sanitation:** According to the 2011 Census, amenities available with the households has been listed as follows: 87% of households are using tap, tube well, hand pump and covered well as the main source of drinking water while 43.5 percent use tap water. Only 47% of households have source of water within the premises while 36% of households have to fetch water from a source located within 500 mts in rural areas/100 mts in urban areas and 17% still fetch drinking water from a source located more than 500 mts away in rural areas or 100 mts in urban area. No city has round the clock water supply in India. Intermittent supply results in a vacuum being created in empty water lines which often suck in pollutants through leaking joints. Many small towns have no main water supply at all and are dependent on the wells. To overcome these problem Municipal bodies must focus on increasing operational efficiencies through reduction in pilferage, improving efficiency of staff and use of technology. Further the municipal bodies should meter all water connection within a time frame. Installing a hierarchy of metering system could help in identifying pilferage.

Drainage situation is equally bad. Around half of the households have drainage connectivity with two-third have the open drainage and one-third has the closed drainage. Because of the non- existence of a drainage system, large pools of stagnant water can be seen in city even in summer months. Further the sanitation problem is also high due to lack of toilet facilities in slums areas. According to the census, 47% of the households have latrine facility within premises with 36% households have water closet and 9%

households have pit latrine. Thus, practice of open defecation is prevalent. Human waste is also responsible for spreading of water borne diseases like typhoid, cholera, shigellosis, amebic dysenteries, diarrhea, etc. The practice of open defecation in India comes from a combination of factors the most prominent of them being the traditional behavioral pattern and lack of awareness of the people about the associated health hazards.

6. **Electronic waste:** A new type of hazardous waste has come up in recent years, namely electronic waste. E-waste consists of all waste from electronic and electrical appliances which have reached their end- of- life period or are no longer fit for their original intended use and are destined for recovery, recycling or disposal. It includes computer and its accessories monitors, printers, keyboards, central processing units; typewriters, mobile phones and chargers, remotes, compact discs, headphones, batteries, LCD/Plasma TVs, air conditioners, refrigerators and other household appliances. The composition of e-waste is diverse and falls under 'hazardous' and 'non-hazardous' categories. Broadly, it consists of ferrous and non-ferrous metals, plastics, glass, wood and plywood, printed circuit boards, concrete, ceramics, rubber and other items. Iron and steel constitute about 50% of the waste, followed by plastics (21%), non-ferrous metals (13%) and other constituents. Non-ferrous metals consist of metals like copper, aluminum and precious metals like silver, gold, platinum, palladium and so on. The presence of elements like lead, mercury, arsenic, cadmium, selenium, hexavalent chromium, and flame retardants beyond threshold quantities make e-waste hazardous in nature. It contains over 1000 different substances, many of which are toxic, and creates serious pollution upon disposal. Obsolete computers pose the most significant environmental and health hazard among the e-wastes. There are 10 States that contribute to 70 per cent of the total e-waste generated in the country, while 65 cities generate more than 60 per cent of the total e-waste in India. Among the 10 largest e-waste generating States, Maharashtra ranks first followed by Tamil Nadu, Andhra Pradesh, Uttar Pradesh, West Bengal, Delhi, Karnataka, Gujarat, Madhya Pradesh and Punjab. Among the top ten cities generating e-waste, Mumbai ranks first followed by Delhi, Bengaluru, Chennai, Kolkata, Ahmedabad, Hyderabad, Pune, Surat and Nagpur. The main sources of electronic waste in India are the government, public and private (industrial) sectors, which account for

almost 70 per cent of total waste generation. The contribution of individual households is relatively small at about 15 per cent; the rest being contributed by manufacturers. Though individual households are not large contributors to waste generated by computers, they consume large quantities of consumer durables and are, therefore, potential creators of waste.

7. **Urban poverty:** Urban poverty is a major challenge before the urban managers and administrators of the present time. Though the anti-poverty strategy comprising of a wide range of poverty alleviation and employment generating programmes has been implemented but results show that the situation is grim. Importantly, poverty in urban India gets exacerbated by substantial rate of population growth, high rate of migration from the rural areas and mushrooming of slum pockets. Migration alone accounts for about 40 per cent of the growth in urban population, converting the rural poverty into urban one. Moreover, poverty has become synonymous with slums. The relationship is bilateral i.e. slums also breed poverty. This vicious circle never ends. Most of the world's poor reside in India and majority of the poor live in rural areas and about one-fourth urban population in India lives below poverty line. If we count those who are deprived of safe drinking water, adequate clothing, or shelter, the number is considerably higher. Further, the vulnerable groups such as Scheduled Castes, Scheduled Tribes, minorities, pavement dwellers etc., are living in acute poverty. Housing conditions in large cities and towns are depicting sub human lives of slum dwellers. With the reconstruction of poverty alleviation programmes in urban India it is expected that social and economic benefits will percolate to the population below the poverty line. However, eradication of poverty and improving the quality of life of the poor remains one of the daunting tasks.

8. **Haphazard growth of cities:** The most important obstacle to sustainable growth of cities is the total lack of regulation of this sector, nowadays; it is laced with black money, red tapes, land mafias and corruption. It is also recognized that existing laws on land registry, transfer of property, contracts and related matters are themselves inadequate in this context and are implemented by different authorities and they cast no responsibility (or liability) on the builder/developer for observing certain core norms in the contracts with home-buyers. In recent years, considerable progress has been made in setting up empowered

regulatory bodies for the financial sector for investments in corporate, companies and mutual funds.

THE SOLUTIONS TO URBANIZATION

To solve the problem of urbanization, we should apply the following solutions:

(a) **To create Employment at Rural Level:** The chief responsible factor for urbanization is limited employment in villages. We should try to create more and more employment in rural areas itself. We should develop agricultural industries, rural industries, forests and rural skills in rural areas so as to provide employment as well as deteriorate the migration towards the cities.

(b) **The Development at Agricultural Level:** The main source of income and employment of villagers is based on farming. But unfortunately, even after 59 years of Economic Planning, we are unable to provide the irrigation facility to the useful land for farming. Where the farming is based only on Monsoon, in such areas, it has become difficult to live in such draughty condition. More development should be made in agriculture in rural areas and if its benefits one reached to the villagers, there will definitely be deterioration in urbanization.

(c) **The Development of Businesses based on Agriculture:** With the development in agriculture in villages, we should start some business based activities on agriculture like animal husbandry, poultry, sowing trees as to provide employment to the villagers in addition to agriculture. It will increase their income and that will change their attitude of migrating towards cities.

(d) **Use of Natural Resources of Villages:** If we can use the natural resources of villages like land, water, jungles, human wealth, animals etc...in sufficient way, the chances for employment can be increased and that will decrease urbanization.

(e) **To Create Modern Services in Villages:** The dearth of city like facilities in villages is one of the reasons for migration. A young man of village, who comes to the city for education, is not ready to go back to his village due to the lack of facilities. Those who have settled in cities are also not ready for the marriage of their daughters in villages for the same reason. The facilities like water, habitat, roads, primary education, primary health centers, 24 hours electricity etc... should be made available in villages. Where ever possible, the facilities like multiplex theatres, modern hotels and entertainment may be provided in rural areas. It will boost employment and there won't be any difference between cities and villages and that will solve the problem of urbanization to a great extent.

SUMMARY:

This is rightly said, that this century is urban century, where more people are living in urban areas. The urbanization concept provides both the challenges and opportunities for every country, although it may not be uniform in every country. In India also, the urban population is increasing in good number, but there exist a problem of infrastructure deficit, which was a big hurdle in the way of providing basic services to the people and also more importantly the economic growth of the country. Thus, it is the right time for our country, to think and act seriously about the negative implications of the urbanization concept, and make it useful for the development of the country. But, urbanization needs to be sustainable in two counts; First, it is needed to equally benefit of all the people in the society viz. socially inclusive and secondly, environmentally sustainable. Also, generally the three important questions needs to be answered by the future study on urbanization are, first question is regarding, 'what does urbanization mean for rural areas needs to be explored'? The second question is 'does urbanization leads to reduction in poverty rate is questionable'? Thirdly, 'are the developing and under-developing countries prepared to handle their urban transition'? The answer to these questions will help us to understand, the urbanization concept very well for the development of any society and people living in it, including India.

GLOSSARY:

1. **Urban:** It relates to, or constituting a city or town. Living in a city or town. (Of music) emerging and developing in densely populated areas of large cities, esp. those populated by people of African or Caribbean origin Compare rural.
2. **Urbanism:** It explains the chief form of the condition of life. It represents a revolutionary change in the whole pattern of social life.

Urbanism is considered as a condition or set to circumstances.

3. **Urbanization:** Urbanization is a shift of people from village to city. If the rate of increase in urban population is just equal or less to the rate of increase in rural population, it might be said that there is no increase in urbanization. In the real sense, if the thinking, ideas and social values are urban, in that situation these people are urbanized in spite living in a village.

4. **Metropolis:** A metropolis is a large city or conurbation which is a significant economic, political, and cultural ... This article is about the political definition of "metropolis".

5. **Town:** A town is a medium-sized human settlement. Towns are generally larger than villages but smaller than cities, though the criteria which constitute them vary considerably in different parts of the world.

6. **Cities:** A city is a large human settlement. Cities generally have extensive systems for housing, transportation, sanitation, utilities, land use, and communication.

CHECK YOUR PROGRESS:

1. Urbanization refers to the increasing growth and development of cities and towns.

2. To check the progress of urbanization, one can examine population data to see how many people are living in urban areas compared to rural ones.

3. A notable trend in urbanization is the migration of people from rural areas to urban centers in search of better economic opportunities and improved living standards.

4. The expansion of infrastructure, such as roads, buildings, and public services, is a key indicator of urbanization progress.

5. Additionally, monitoring the rate of urbanization, which is the percentage of a country's population living in urban areas, helps track the ongoing trend.

REFERENCES:

1. Census of India: 1961,1971,1981,1991,2001,2011

2. Singh, R.L. (1973); Urban Geography in Developing Countries. NGSI: Varanasi
3. Mishra, R.P. and K. Mishra (1988); Million Cities in India. New Delhi
4. Despande, S.andDespande, L. (1998) " Impact of Liberalisation of Labour Market in India

:What Do Facts from NSSO's 50th Round Show" Economic and Political Weekly, Vol.33No 22,ppL21-L31

5. Kundu, A (1983): "Theories of City Size Distribution and Indian Urban Structure –

AReappraisal", Economic and Political weekly, 18(3).

6. Premi, M. K. (1991): "India's Urban Scene and Its Future Implications", Demography India,20(1)
7. Registrar General (1991) Census of India , Emerging Trends of Urbanisation in India,Occasional paper No. 1 of 1993, Registrar General, New Delhi
8. Registrar General, 2001: Census of India, 2001, India, 2A, Mansingh Road, New Delhi110011, 25th July, 2001
9. Sen, A. and Ghosh, J. (1993): Trends in Rural Employment and Poverty Employment Linkage,ILO-ARTEP Working Paper, New Delhi
10. Sovani, N. V. (1966): Urbanisation and Urban India, Asia Publishing House, Bombay

TERMINAL QUESTIONS:

A. **Long Questions:**

1. Examine the trends of urbanization in India from the mid of 19th century to till to date.

2. India has observed the rapid growth rate of urbanization during the last three decades. Clarify.
3. Examine the contribution of large cities in the urbanization of India.
4. India has a slow pace of urbanization. Clarify this statement.
5. Write an essay on urban region of India.
6. Discuss the problems associated with Indian urbanization.
7. Discuss the main areas of urban concentration in India.

B. Short Questions

1. What is urbanization?
2. What are the main drivers of urbanization?
3. What percentage of India's population is currently living in urban areas?
4. How has the rate of urbanization in India changed over the past few decades?
5. What are the challenges associated with rapid urbanization in India?
6. Can you name some of the major metropolitan cities in India that have experienced significant urban growth?
7. How does urbanization affect the demand for basic services like housing, healthcare, and education in India?
8. What government initiatives or policies are in place to manage urbanization and its impact on India?
9. How does urbanization impact employment patterns and opportunities in India?
10. What are some of the potential benefits of urbanization for India's economy and society?

C. Multiple choice questions

1. What is urbanization?

A. The growth of rural areas
B. The increase in urban population
C. The expansion of forests
D. The development of highways (Answer: B)

2. Which of the following is a primary driver of urbanization in India?

A. Decreasing job opportunities in cities
B. Growth of agriculture in rural areas
C. Industrialization and economic development
D. Strict government policies limiting urban growth (Answer: C)

3. What is the approximate urban population percentage in India as of 2021

A. 30%, B. 50%, C. 70%, D. 90% (Answer: B)

4. Which of the following regions in India has the highest level of urbanization?

A. Northern India

B. Southern India

C. Western India

D. Eastern India (Answer: C)

5. What is the trend of rural-to-urban migration in India?

A. It has significantly decreased in recent years.
B. It has remained relatively constant.
C. It has steadily increased over time.
D. It is negligible and not relevant. (Answer: C)

6. Which city is often referred to as the "Financial Capital of India" and is a significant urban center?

A. New Delhi
B. Kolkata
C. Mumbai
D. Chennai (Answer: C)

7. Which of the following is a common issue associated with rapid urbanization in India?

A. Increased agricultural production
B. Decreased air pollution
C. Slums and inadequate housing
D. Abundant natural resources (Answer: C)

8. What is the Smart Cities Mission in India aimed at achieving?

A. Developing cities with advanced technology only
B. Promoting sustainable urban development and improving quality of life
C. Building more shopping malls in urban areas
D. Reducing urban population through migration policies (Answer: B)

9. Which government agency is responsible for urban planning and development in India?

A. Indian Space Research Organization (ISRO)
B. Ministry of Urban Development
C. Department of Agriculture
D. Indian Railway Corporation (Answer: B)

10. What is the impact of urbanization on the environment?

A. Reduced strain on natural resources
B. Increased green spaces and forests in cities
C. Elevated pollution levels and pressure on resources
D. Preservation of wildlife habitats (Answer: C)

CHAPTER THREE

TRIBAL AREAS

INTRODUCTION

The tribal are the economically backward ethnic group in India. They are food gathers, hunters, forestland cultivators, and minor forest product collectors. They lived in isolation with near to nature hence, called son of soil. Tribes constituted separate socio-cultural groups having distinct customs, tradition, marriage, kinship, property inheritance system and living largely in agricultural and pre-agricultural level of technology (Nagada, 2004).

Article 366 (25) of the Constitution of India refers to Scheduled Tribes as those communities, who are scheduled in accordance with Article 342 of the Constitution. This Article says that only those communities who have been declared as such by the President through an initial public notification or through a subsequent amending Act of Parliament will be considered to be Scheduled Tribes.

Fig. 3.1: Showcasing Tribes in India

India is a home of number of tribes there are over 314 communities. Tribal society as define as a collection of families bearing a common name, speaking a common dialect, occupying a common territory. Simple the word tribe means a group of families, living in a contiguous region, speaking a common language and having a historical past. The constitution of India provides a definition. According, articles 342 of constitution of India, the scheduled tribes are the tribes or communities, which have been declared as such by the President of India.

India has a large mass which shelters different varieties of human races. The incoming of these races started since early Paleolithic period through the mountain passes of the north-west which provided ancient land routes to India. New immigrants pushed early settlers south and eastwards to interior part of the country. Many foreign invaders coming from the north-west although returned to their homeland with plundered booty but some of them decided to settle back here. All these helped in the formation of mixed racial characteristics in the country. So, much so that India has a unique assemblage of human races rarely seen elsewhere in the world.

Although majority of the scholars believe that earlier human races migrated to India from Africa, Mediterranean, West Asia and Central Asia but a group of anthropologist consider India as the cradle land for a number of human races from where they migrated to Sri Lanka, Malaysia, Indonesia, Thailand, Australia and Africa. Paleontology and researchers have given evidences that Siwalik area has been the home of early human ancestors. According to Haddon Pre-Dravidian were the first to occupy this territory. P. Mitra considers Proto-Negroid to be the first settlers, while D.N. Mazumdar gives this credit to Proto-Australoids. According to B.S. Guha, Negrito races were the first to appear on this land and were followed by Proto-Australoids, Pre- Dravidians, Mediterranean's and Nordics.

TRIBAL AREAS AND THEIR PROBLEMS

Indian tribes and their classification:

Sir Herbert Risley (1901) was the first scholars to present a lucid description of the Indian races and their origin. Taking into account the linguistic, cultural and racial attributes he classified India's races into seven major categories.

<u>Classification of Indian Races by Herbert Risley.</u>

1. **Turko-Iranian:** Afghan, Baluchi: Baluchistan, North West Frontier Province area of Pakistan
2. **Indo-Aryan:** Rajput, Khatri, Jat: Rajasthan, Punjab, Kashmir Valley.
3. **Scytho- Dravidian:** Nagar Brahman, Maratha Kumbis, Coorgis: Gujarat, Maharashtra, South-West Sindh
4. **Arya- Dravidian:** Indo-Aryan, Dravidian: Uttar Pradesh, Bihar, East Rajasthan.
5. **Monglo- Dravidian:** Bengali: West Bengal, Coastal Orissa.
6. **Mongoloid:** Palaeo, Tibeto: Himalayan Region, Nepal, Assam, Sikkim.

7. **Dravidian:** Palaeo Dravidians: Tamil Nadu, Andhra Pradesh, Kerala, Madhya Pradesh.

This classification could not gain popularity because it does not take into account the physical/hereditary characteristics of human races. It is mainly based on such elements like language and culture which are not very much related to the racial characteristics. Risley also not mentioned the Negrito race whose representative are seen in Kochi, Hills of the south India, Andaman and Nicobar, Lakshadweep and Maldives.

India contains an unparalleled variety of ethnic groups, patterns of culture and modes of living. "The People of India" a Project of the Anthropological Survey of India has identified about 461 tribal communities of India out of which 174 have been identified as sub-groups. They number about 67,758,000 according to the 1991 Census comprising about 8.01 per cent of the total population of the country. In this Unit we will look into the distributional patterns of the tribes of India. Even though there is not a single and definite system of classifying the tribes of India, attempts have been made by different anthropologists from time to time to distribute the tribes. There are mainly two categories to classify the tribes. They are:

I. Permanent traits: This includes factors like geography/ territory, language, physical/racial attributes and size.
II. Non- Permanent or acquired traits: This includes factors like economy or subsistence pattern and the degree of incorporation into the Hindu society.

Geographical: The tribes of India are dispersed widely over geographical territory and scholars have attempted to arrange them along the regions they inhabit. Based on the geographical location and the tribal demographical set-up, anthropologists have tried to chalk out a zonal classification or a regional grouping of the tribes of India. For instance, B.S. Guha has classified the tribes of India into three zones:

1. The north and north-eastern zone in the mountain valleys and eastern frontiers of India.
2. The central or middle zone occupying the older hills and plateaus along the dividing line between the Peninsular India and the Indo-Gangetic

Plains including the converging line of the Western Ghats.
3. The southern zone comprising the whole of the Peninsular India.

D.N. Majumdar and T.N. Madan in their book 'Introduction to Social Anthropology' have also offered a similar classification. They are Northern and North-Eastern Zone, the Central or Middle Zone and the Southern Zone.

S.C. Dube has demarcated four geographical regions including the North and North- Eastern Zone, Middle Zone, the South Zone and the West Zone. Taking into consideration the zonal classification given by different anthropologists from time to time and keeping in mind the geographical, ecological, socio-economic, administrative, ethnic and racial factors, L.P.Vidyarthi put forward a five-fold classification system which included the following: the Himalayan region, Middle India, Western India, South India and the Islands.

<u>The Himalayan region is sub-divided into:</u>

A) North-eastern Himalayan region comprising the states of Assam, Meghalaya, Arunachal Pradesh, Nagaland, Manipur, Mizoram, Tripura and the mountainous region of West Bengal including Darjeeling.

B) Central Himalayan region comprising the Terai (the strip of land joining the plains to the mountains) areas of Uttar Pradesh and Bihar and

C) North-Western Himalayan region comprising the states of Himachal Pradesh and Jammu and Kashmir. The tribes inhabiting this region are the Akas, Daflas, Apatanis, Mishmis, Khamptis, Singphos, Kukis, Khasis, Garos, Lepchas, Bhotias, Tharus, etc.

Middle India Region comprising the states of Bihar, West Bengal, Orissa and Madhya Pradesh. About 55% of the total tribal population of the country lives in this region. The tribes inhabiting this region are the Juangs, Kharia, Khonds, Bhumijs, Baiga, Muria, Marias, Mundas, Gonds, Santhals, Oraons, etc.

Western India Region comprising the states of Rajasthan, Gujarat, Maharashtra, Goa and the Union Territory of Dadra and Nagar Haveli. The tribes inhabiting this region are the Barodias, Bharwads, Bhils, Damors, Dhanwars, Dhodias, Girasias, Gonds, Katkaris, Koknas, Kolis, Minas, Siddi, Warlis, etc.

South India Region comprising the states of Andhra Pradesh, Tamil Nadu, Karnataka and Kerala. The tribes inhabiting this region are the Chenchus, Irulas, Paniyans, Kurumbas, Kadars, Todas, Badagas, Kotas, etc.

The Island Region comprising the islands of Andaman and Nicobar in the Bay of Bengal and Lakshadweep in the Arabian Sea. The tribes inhabiting this region are the Jarwas, Onges, the Great Andamanese, North Sentinelese, etc.

K.S. Singh has offered a similar classification of tribes of India into the Northeastern India, Middle India, Southern India, North-western Himalayas, and Andaman and Nicobar Islands Zones. Within this geographical classification, there is a lot of disparity in regards to the distribution of the tribal population of the country. A very high concentration of the tribal population in the eight states of the central or middle India comprising of about 85 percent of the total tribal population. This is followed by the eight north-eastern states comprising of about 11 percent while the rest is distributed over the states and union territories of the northern and southern India.

Linguistic: Besides classifying the tribes according to territory, they are also classified according to language or linguistic categories. Four broad language groups have been identified amongst the tribes of India which are Indo-Aryan, Austro-Asiatic, Dravidian and Tibeto-Burman. Tracing the linguistic map of India, we can see that the tribal people of India speak different languages in different regions and groups. One can find that the Dravidian language is spoken in southern India and in some pockets in central India; the Austro-Asiatic language is spoken in some pockets in the north-eastern Himalayan region of Meghalaya, in Nicobar Islands and most part of central India; the Tibeto-Burman language is spoken in the entire Himalayan region whereas the Indo-Aryan language is spoken in the remaining areas of the rest of the country. L.P Vidyarthi and Binay Kumar Rai in their book "The Tribal Culture of India" put forward a classificatory system of the languages of Indian tribes: Dravidian, Austro-Asiatic, Tibeto-Chinese, Indo-Aryan.

Racial: On the basis of the physical attributes, anthropologists have tried to categories the tribal population from time to time. But due to the lack of available knowledge and scanty direct evidence, the determination of the racial genesis and affinities of the tribal communities of India is a very complicated task. The first attempt to categories the Indian tribal communities in a scientific manner based on the racial characteristics was done by Sir Herbert Risley. He classified the entire population of the country into seven racial types which are Turko Iranian, Indo-Aryan, Scytho-Dravidian, Aryo-Dravidian, Mongolo-Dravidian, Mongoloid and the

Dravidian.

No separate classificatory scheme for the tribal population was given. A more recent attempt of classification was given by J.H. Hutton, S.C. Guha and D.N. Majumdar out of which the most accepted classification is that offered by S.C. Guha who listed six main races with nine sub-types. They are as follows:

1. Negrito
2. Proto- Australoid
3. Mongoloid A) Paleo-Mongoloids- Long-headed and Broad-headed B) Tibeto-Mogoloids
4. Mediterranean A) Palaeo- Mediterranean B) Mediterranean C) Oriental type
5. Western Brachycephals A) Alpinoid B) Dinaric C) Armenoid
6. Nordic Guha has also drawn conclusions as regards to the racial composition of the tribes of India. They are: I) Negrito: 30 Tribal Cosmogenies II) Proto-Australoid III) Mongoloid

Size: Anthropologists have also attempted to classify the tribal groups according to their demographic size. It is interesting to note that tribal populations of India vary immensely with regards to their respective sizes. On one hand we find tribal communities like the Gonds, Bhils, (both designated with their generic names) with a population of about forty lakhs each followed by the Santhals with a population of more than thirty lakhs. They are followed by the Oraons, Minas and the Mundas who number about more than ten lakhs each. They are followed by the Hos, Khonds and the Kols with population strength of more than five lakhs. Yet another more than forty tribes, comprising about ten percent of the total tribal population of India have a population ranging from one to five lakhs. These are the Adis, Baigas, Bhumijs, Bodos-Kacharis, Dhodias, Garos, Kacharis, Kharias, Kharwars, Khasis, Kolhas, Korkus, Lodhas, Mizos, Rabhas, Saoras, Tripuris, Warlis, Yenadis and Yerukulas,to name a few. On the contrary there are communities like some Andamanese groups who number even less than hundred each. There is a lot of variation in size even within the tribal groups who lie in between these two categories- somewhere from between less than 1000 to less than a million.

Economy or Subsistence Pattern: On the basis of the mode of livelihood or the subsistence pattern, Indian tribes can be divided into:

1. Food gatherers and hunters
2. Horticulturists
3. Pastoralists
4. Hill cultivation type
5. Agriculturists
6. Simple Artisan
7. Folk Artist
8. Laborers and
9. Industrial workers

DISTRIBUTION OF TRIBES IN INDIA

India is having second largest concentration of tribal population in the world. There are over 314 tribal communities in India, known by different names such as the Adivasis- the original inhabitants, Vanya Jati (live in forest), Adim Jati- primitive people, etc. Tribals are most backward community in India. The Indian tribes display a very high degree of ethnic diversity both in their racial composition and dialectal and linguistic affinity. There are 285 different tribal communities, which show an important index of their ethnic diversity. No less impressive is the pattern of their spatial distribution, it has been commonly observed that the tribes reveal strong tendencies of clustering and concentration in the hilly, forested and the geographically inaccessible tracts of the country (Ahmad, 1999). This is the main cause for their backwardness.

Tribal population is concentrated in geographically inaccessible areas so one can say development of tribals mostly depends on the distribution of population in relation to resource available in the region. Population and the natural resources are the most important aspects of regional development. In this context growth and distribution of tribal population is an important aspect (Ramotra and Mote, 2009).

In Spatial and cultural consideration Indian scheduled tribe population is at widely different stage of social, cultural, political as well as economic development. The scheduled tribes account for a sizeable proportion of the population of India. They constitute an important segment of the Indian social fabric. These communities belong to different ethno-lingual groups and profess diverse faiths. Living at disparate levels of socio-economic development, they are spread along the entire spectrum of social evolution in India ranging from the industrial workers (Raza and Ahmad, 1990). As per the 1991 census the scheduled tribe population in India was

6.78 crores, which constituted about 8.01 per cent of the total population. According to 2001 census the scheduled tribes constituted about 8 per cent in India.

The largest concentration of scheduled tribe is confined to central India particularly in Madhya Pradesh and in its adjoining states like Maharashtra, Gujarat, Rajasthan, Andhra Pradesh, Zarkhand, Orissa and Bihar. In Maharashtra the scheduled tribe population was 73.18 lakhs (1991), which constituted 9.27 per cent of the total population of the state. It has now increased to 85.77 lakhs in 2001 but the proportion has reduced to 8.85 per cent. In Maharashtra concentration of tribal population is mostly confined to north-eastern and north western parts. In the north-western part of the state particularly Thane, Nashik, Dhule and Nandurbar districts where more than 43.

The tribal population of the country, as per 2011 census, is 10.43 crore, constituting 8.6% of the total population. 89.97% of them live in rural areas and 10.03% in urban areas. The decadal population growth of the tribe's from Census 2001 to 2011 has been 23.66% against the 17.69% of the entire population. 9 per cent concentration of tribal population in the state is concentrated (2001).

The trend in ST population since Census 1961 is illustrated in Table 3.1. From 30.1 million in 1961, the ST population has increased to 104.3 million in 2011.

Year	Total Population	Scheduled Tribes	Proportion of STs
1961	439.2	30.1	6.9
1971	547.9	38.0	6.9
1981	665.3	51.6	7.8
1991	838.6	67.8	8.1
2001	1028.6	84.3	8.2
2011	1210.8	104.3	8.6

Table 3.1: Trends in Proportion of Scheduled Tribe Population.*Source: Census of India*

Broadly the STs inhabit two distinct geographical areas – the Central India and the North- Eastern Area. More than half of the Scheduled Tribe population is concentrated in Central India, i.e., Madhya Pradesh (14.69%), Chhattisgarh (7.5%), Jharkhand (8.29%), Andhra Pradesh (5.7%), Maharashtra (10.08%), Orissa (9.2%), Gujarat (8.55%) and Rajasthan

(8.86%). The other distinct area is the North East (Assam, Nagaland, Mizoram, Manipur, Meghalaya, Tripura, Sikkim and Arunachal Pradesh).

It can be observed that more than two-third of the ST population is concentrated only in the seven States of the country, viz. Madhya Pradesh, Maharashtra, Orissa, Gujarat, Rajasthan, Jharkhand and Chhattisgarh. There is no ST population in three States (Delhi NCR, Punjab and Haryana) and two UTs (Puducherry and Chandigarh), as no Scheduled tribe is notified. Among States, Mizoram has the highest proportion of Scheduled Tribes (94.43) and Uttar Pradesh has the lowest proportion of Scheduled Tribes (0.57).

States and 2 UTs have higher percentage of ST population than country's average of 8.6%. Table 4 gives State-wise comparison of Absolute number of All Population and Tribal Population in terms of Total, Male & Female and Table 5 gives the State-wise Tribal Population and decadal change by residence (Total, Rural & Urban) as per Census 2011.

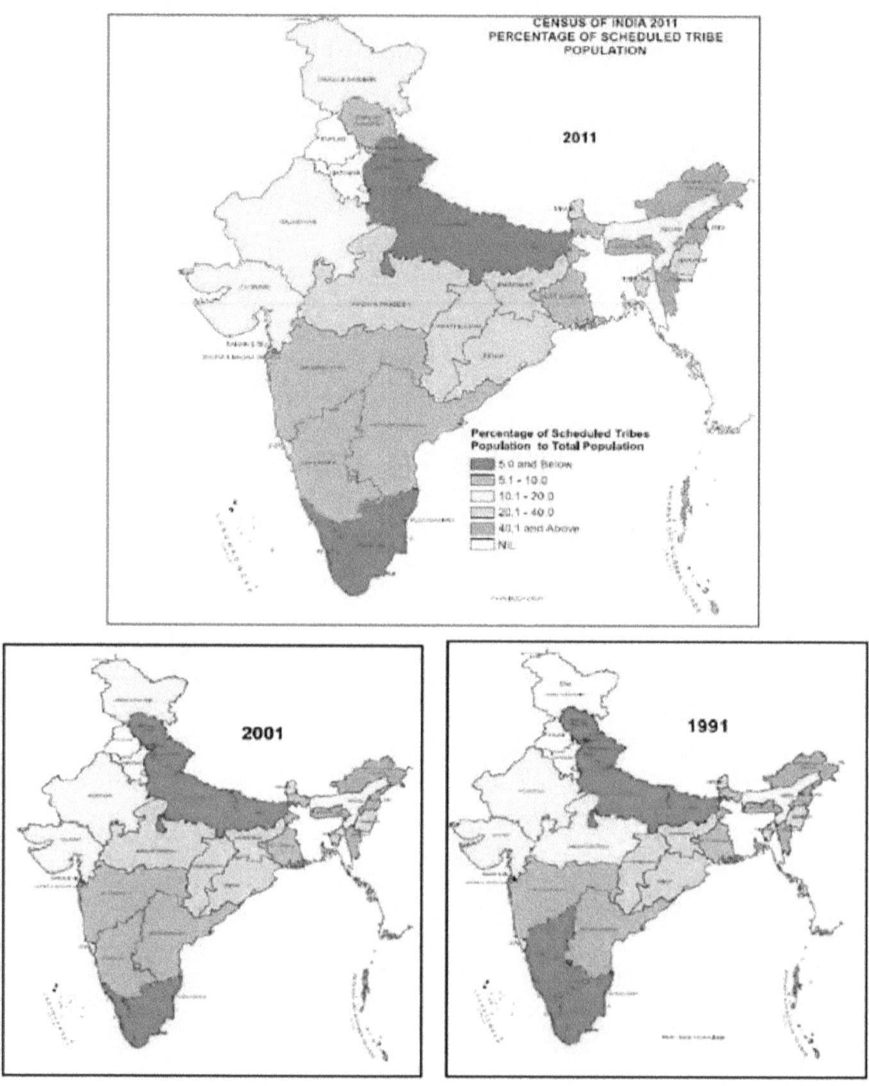

Figure 3.2 Spatial Distribution of Tribes in Indian States.

The data reveals that at all India level a decline of 32 percent is observed in the hundred percent groups of tribal villages. Among the states, maximum decline is noticed in Manipur, Meghalaya, Assam, Nagaland, Madhya Pradesh and Odisha in this category. In the next category of 90-100 tribal villages 5 percent rise is seen over the period 2001 to 2011.This is due to small rises in practically all the states. In the 75-90 group there is a marginal increase of 5 percent over the period 2001 to 2011 and the trend of state-wise distribution is similar to the previous group. In the next two groups of tribal villages 50-75 and 25-50 the state-wise features and the all India growth pattern is more or less of the same order observed in the previous groups. Thus a significant feature that emerges during the period 2001 to 2011 is the decline in 100 percent tribal villages with marginal increases in the other classes of tribal villages.

STATE LEVEL DISTRIBUTION OF TRIBES IN INDIA

Since the tribes display a high tendency of clustering and concentration in the hilly and forested tracts of the country, they are highly unevenly distributed between the states of the Indian Union. On the basis of relief, the states and the union territories may be grouped into two categories: (a) those characterized by rugged topography, and (b) those with an open relief, (plains and river valleys).

The tribes are heavily concentrated in the former and not in the latter. For example, Punjab, Haryana, Chandigarh, Delhi and Uttar Pradesh, which lie over the Indo- Gangetic plain and have a rich agricultural base, belong to the second category. They have either no tribal population or else the numerical strength of tribal population is negligible. In Uttar Pradesh, for example, the tribes are mostly concentrated in the hilly districts of Uttarakhand. Likewise, the tribes are either non-existent or their population is negligible over the plains of Bihar and West Bengal. On the other hand, tribes have a strong presence in the plateau region of southern Bihar. They are also predominant in the hilly districts of north Bengal as well as over the plateau districts of the states bordering on Bihar. Assam, despite being an extension of the North Indian Plain, supports a large chunk of tribal population. In fact, every eighth Assamese is a tribal. The southern states of Kerala, Karnataka, Tamil Nadu and Andhra Pradesh lie mostly in the plateau region and yet the population of tribes in these states is not very large. It varies from 1.03 per cent in Tamil Nadu to 6.31 per cent in Andhra Pradesh.

The tribes are, however, numerically strong in the central Indian states from Gujarat and Maharashtra to Orissa and Bihar. Among them Madhya Pradesh has the highest proportion of tribal population, i.e., 23.27 per cent of the state's population, followed by Orissa (22.21 per cent), Gujarat (14.92 per cent), Rajasthan (12.44 percent), Bihar (7.66 percent) and West Bengal (5.60 percent).

State	100% Tribals		> 90% Tribals		> 75% Tribals		> 50% Tribals		> 25% Tribals	
	2001	2011	2001	2011	2001	2011	2001	2011	2001	2011
Jammu & Kashmir	157	89	358	369	460	488	711	766	1168	1295
Himachal Pradesh	248	230	444	490	611	682	808	966	1011	1411
Punjab	-	-	-	-	-	-	-	-	-	-
Chandigarh	-	-	-	-	-	-	-	-	-	-
Uttarakhand	42	35	102	85	234	174	461	419	650	640
Haryana	-	-	-	-	-	-	-	-	-	-
Delhi	-	-	-	-	-	-	-	-	-	-
Rajasthan	1538	1152	3468	4456	4820	5701	6872	7763	9571	10654
Uttar Pradesh	20	23	49	124	63	197	74	340	93	623
Bihar	177	98	287	295	399	447	611	720	989	1155
Sikkim	4	2	12	17	36	51	77	138	178	285
Arunachal Pradesh	2165	2382	2894	3929	3144	4367	3378	4667	3555	4859
Nagaland	551	215	1105	1136	1201	1265	1247	1351	1271	1388
Manipur	1244	554	1586	1741	1663	1844	1694	1887	1722	1905
Mizoram	370	130	642	651	677	684	697	699	702	700
Tripura	123	22	302	301	377	385	451	466	549	564
Meghalaya	3944	1890	5257	5867	5460	6099	5575	6205	5621	6262
Assam	2772	1503	4309	4562	5107	5406	6311	6626	7689	8066
West Bengal	992	711	1601	1629	2302	2357	3900	3977	7256	7454
Jharkhand	3317	2451	6291	6370	8870	9008	12118	12239	15015	15171
Odisha	5085	3839	8688	8684	12249	12396	17531	17798	23000	23208
Chandigarh	1083	1076	3242	3200	5956	5926	9441	9418	12392	12298
Madhya Pradesh	2670	1619	7412	7338	10714	10687	14927	15022	20780	20927
Gujarat	1345	935	3446	3531	4007	4089	4934	4970	6089	6085
Daman & Diu	-	-	3	2	3	3	5	5	8	9
Dadra & Nagar Haveli	9	5	43	44	56	57	63	62	70	64
Maharashtra	1214	930	3614	3760	4785	4836	6640	6738	9944	10257
Andhra Pradesh	2407	1466	3812	3928	4444	4515	5239	5335	6589	6748
Karnataka	78	61	224	224	438	447	1032	1083	2799	3000
Goa	-	2	-	11	-	19	-	38	-	78
Lakshadweep	-	1	7	4	8	5	8	5	8	6
Kerala	-	-	-	-	-	-	5	6	25	26
Tamilnadu	75	46	210	231	267	282	323	320	391	391
Pondicherry	-	-	-	-	-	-	-	-	-	-
A&N Islands	112	41	141	77	157	84	163	89	167	93
All India	31742	21508	59549	63056	78508	82501	105296	110118	139302	145622

Source:Census of india 2001,2011

Table 3.2: State wise Distribution of tribal villages by Different Concentration of Groups.

The northeastern states stand out as a category in themselves as the population in these states is predominantly tribal, although the numerical strength of tribes is not very large. Tribal proportion is particularly high in Mizoram, Nagaland and Meghalaya (85-95 per cent) and significantly high in Arunachal Pradesh (64 per cent). On the other hand, about one-third of the population in Tripura and Manipur consists of tribes. The share of tribal population is overwhelmingly large in certain union territories, such as Dadra and Nagar Haveli and Lakshadweep. On the contrary, the proportion of tribes in the population of Andaman and Nicobar Islands is insignificant. (Table 3.2).

Evidently, tribal communities have either by their choice favored concentration in inhospitable environments, or conversely the peasant societies have pushed them and confined them to these enclaves thus having free access to the potentially rich lands suited pre-eminently to the agricultural pursuits. This, by and large, mutual exclusivity of the tribal and the peasant modes is an important attribute of spatial distribution of social categories in India.

decile limit*	district count		tehsil count		village count	
	2001	2011	2001	2011	2001	2011
0 - 10	356	369	3479	3596	415443	411663
10 - 20	75	74	598	626	28661	29800
20 - 30	31	42	274	337	18735	19299
30 - 40	19	24	153	199	13954	14601
40 - 50	18	21	145	164	11554	12002
50 - 60	18	16	131	158	10771	11332
60 - 70	14	17	139	175	10513	10729
70 - 80	13	16	115	131	11167	11400
80 - 90	9	16	103	141	13296	13601
90 -&above	31	45	275	458	59549	63056
All	584	640[@]	5412	5985[@]	593643	597483

Lower limit included   *Source: Census 2001,2011*

[@] There are 9 district and 106 tehsils with no rural poplulations

Table 3.3: Number of Districts, Tehsil and Villages in Different Deciles Groups.

It may be observed that the tribes are conspicuous by their absence in 36 districts mostly lying over the North Indian Plain. As noted earlier, the states of Punjab, Haryana, and the union territory of Chandigarh as well as the National Capital Territory of Delhi have no scheduled tribes as such. This is anomalous. They may be found there as immigrants but not recognized as scheduled tribes. The other states of the North Indian Plain, viz., Uttar Pradesh, northern and central parts of Bihar and West Bengal generally follow the same pattern with tribal share in population being negligible, less than one percent. This means that over most of Uttar Pradesh groups or individuals may be enumerated as tribes, even though their status may be in-migrant. This is also true for the alluvial plains of Bihar and West Bengal.

List of Major Tribes in India: State Wise

1. **Andhra Pradesh:** Andh, Sadhu Andh, Bhagata, Bhil, Chenchus (Chenchawar), Gadabas, Gond, Goundu, Jatapus, Kammara, Kattunayakan, Kolawar, Kolam, Konda, Manna Dhora, Pardhan, Rona, Savaras, Dabba Yerukula, Nakkala, Dhulia, Thoti, Sugalis.

2. **Arunachal Pradesh:** Apatanis, Abor, Dafla, Galong, Momba, Sherdukpen, Singpho.

3. **Assam:** Chakma, Chutiya, Dimasa, Hajong, Garos, Khasis, Gangte.

4. **Bihar:** Asur, Baiga, Birhor, Birjia, Chero, Gond, Parhaiya, Santhals, Savar.

5. **Chhattisgarh:** Agariya, Bhaina, Bhattra, Biar, Khond, Mawasi, Nagasia.

6. **Goa:** Dhodia, Dubia, Naikda, Siddi,Varli.

7. **Gujarat:** Barda, Bamcha, Bhil, Charan, Dhodia, Gamta, Paradhi, Patelia.

8. **Himachal Pradesh:** Gaddis, Gujjars, Khas, Lamba, Lahaulas, Pangwala, Swangla.

9. **Jammu and Kashmir:** Bakarwal, Balti, Beda, Gaddi, Garra, Mon, Purigpa, Sippi.

10. **Jharkhand:** Birhors, Bhumij, Gonds, Kharia, Mundas, Santhals, Savar.

11. **Karnataka:** Adiyan, Barda, Gond, Bhil, Iruliga, Koraga, Patelia, Yerava.

12. **Kerala:** Adiyan, Arandan, Eravallan, Kurumbas, Malai arayan, Moplahs, Uralis.

13. **Madhya Pradesh:** Baigas, Bhils, Bharia, Birhors, Gonds,Katkari, kharia, Khond, Kol, Murias.

14. **Maharashtra:** Bhaina, Bhunjia, Dhodia, Katkari, Khond, Rathawa, Warlis.

15. **Manipur:** Aimol, Angami, Chiru, Kuki, Maram, Monsang, Paite, Purum, Thadou.

16. **Meghalaya:** Chakma, Garos, Hajong, Jaintias Khasis, Lakher, Pawai, Raba.

17. **Mizoram:** Chakma, Dimasa, Khasi, Kuki, Lakher, Pawai, Raba, Synteng.

18. **Nagaland:** Angami, Garo, Kachari, Kuki, Mikir, Nagas, Sema.

19. **Odisha:** Gadaba, Ghara, Kharia, Khond, Matya, Oraons, Rajuar, Santhals.

20. **Rajasthan:** Bhils, Damaria, Dhanka, Meenas(Minas), Patelia, Sahariya.

21. **Sikkim:** Bhutia, Khas, Lepchas.

22. **Tamil Nadu:** Adiyan, Aranadan, Eravallan, Irular, Kadar, Kanikar, Kotas, Todas.

23. **Telangana:** Chenchus.

24. **Tripura:** Bhil, Bhutia, Chaimal, Chakma, Halam, Khasia, Lushai, Mizel, Namte.

25. **Uttarakhand:** Bhotias, Buksa, Jannsari, Khas, Raji, Tharu.

26. **Uttar Pradesh:** Bhotia, Buksa, Jaunsari, Kol, Raji, Tharu.

27. **West Bengal:** Asur, Khond, Hajong, Ho, Parhaiya, Rabha, Santhals, Savar.

28. **Andaman and Nicobar:** Oraons, Onges, Sentinelese, Shompens.

29. **Little Andaman:** Jarawa.

30. **North-East:** Abhors, Chang, Galaong, Mishimi, Singpho, Wancho.

DOMINANCE AND DISPERSION

There are 24 districts in which the tribal share in population is overwhelmingly large; in fact, the tribes are in a dominant position. Twenty-one of them lie in the northeast. The remaining three districts are situated in Madhya Pradesh Jhabua, Gujarat (Dangs) and Lakshadweep.

Closer to these districts of high dominance is another set of 27 districts in which the tribes have a majority in the district populations, i.e., 50-80 per cent. Many of them are contiguous to the districts of the first category. The geographical distribution is somewhat different. For example, 14 of them are situated outside the northeast. They lie in the states of Bihar, Orissa, Madhya Pradesh, Rajasthan, Gujarat and Himachal Pradesh as well as in the union territories of Dadra and Nagar Haveli and the Andaman and Nicobar Islands. These districts include Dadra and Nagar Haveli (UT), Lahaul and Spiti (Himachal Pradesh), Banswara (Rajasthan), Gumla (Bihar), Bastar (Madhya Pradesh), Dungarpur (Rajasthan), Nicobars (UT), Mandla (Madhya Pradesh), Mayurbhanj (Orissa), Lohardaga (Bihar), Kinnaur (Himachal Pradesh), Pashchimi Singhbhum (Bihar), Valsad (Gujarat), Koraput (Orrisa), Sarguja, Dhar (Madhya Pradesh) and Sundargarh (Orissa).

Together these 51 districts share among themselves 27 per cent of the country's tribal population. These tribal majority districts outside the tribal states of the northeast deserve special reference.

RURAL-URBAN DISTRIBUTIONS

Tribes are mostly a rural phenomenon. This is evident from the fact that about 93 per cent of the tribal population lives in rural areas. Bihar is closest to this national average. States which lie above the national average include Uttar Pradesh, Arunachal Pradesh, Orissa, West Bengal, Madhya Pradesh, Rajasthan, Kerala, Assam, Himachal Pradesh and Tripura. The tribes of Tripura are almost wholly rural as 98 per cent of their population is concentrated in villages. This high rural proportion shows that the tribes are mostly engaged in primary economic activity and they are naturally located in the rural areas. On the other end of the scale is Mizoram with only about one- half of its tribal population being rural. The tribal population in Tamil Nadu, Nagaland, Maharashtra, Meghalaya and Karnataka is largely rural, with the rural proportion ranging between 85 and 87 per cent. It is only in Mizoram that the tribes have been significantly drawn into the urban way of life.

Even though the proportion of urbanized tribes is low in general, their numerical strength is sizeable i.e. more than five million as in 2011. About one-half of this population was living in the cities and towns of Maharashtra, Madhya Pradesh, Gujarat and Bihar alone. In terms of the numerical strength of urban tribes, Maharashtra holds the first rank, followed by Madhya Pradesh, Gujarat and Bihar. Then, there is the case of northeastern states where, as in Mizoram, the urban proportion is high, although the absolute urban population is low in comparison to the mid-Indian states. Tribal urbanization may be seen as an example of rural push rather than urban pull. Mizoram, of course, is an exception. In other states of the country like their non- tribal counterparts, the tribes have been pushed into the urban domain by largely unfavorable conditions prevailing in the home villages. These include deteriorating man-land ratio, caused by land alienation, stringent forest policies denying the tribes their natural right to the forest, location of big or small river valley/industrial projects in tribal areas leading to displacement and the emergence of contractor-ship in the tribal labor market. Thus, a chunk of the urbanized tribes in an Indian city may consist of contractual laborers as well as those ousted from the development project sites. There is evidence to show that the urban economies have accommodated the tribes only marginally. They are mostly unskilled laborers engaged in low- paid jobs and living in squatter colonies. In the city they are perhaps the poorest among the poor. The towns in the North-east may be an exception to this generalization.

PROBLEM OF TRIBAL AREAS

1. **Problems with Land Alienation:** Land as a prime resource has been a source of problem in tribal life because of two related reasons, first, Dependency, i.e. tribal dependency on land and second, improper planning from government agencies. Tribal people in India can be classified on the basis of their economic pursuits in the following way: Foragers, Pastoral, Handicraft makers, Agriculturists, Shifting hill cultivators, Laborers and Business pursuits. All of these occupations involve direct or indirect dependency on land. Land rights and changes in rules go unnoticed. Tribal are unaware or are made unaware about the rules which governs India's land rights. The tribe's do not have access to land records, not even the Record of Rights. This lends them to a higher probability of getting exploited, by the non-tribal and in some cases by the local officials.

Wherever lands are given yet the pattas are not given, or pattas handed over yet the land is not shown. There is a discrepancy in demarcation of Scheduled Areas. In some places, it is village wise and in some places, it is area wise. There should be a clear village-wise demarcation of the Scheduled Area to avoid ambiguities and exploitation of tribal lands. Some of the tribal villages surrounding the Scheduled Areas are administratively called the Tribal Sub-Plan Areas, where land alienation is high and has numerous pending cases. Land restoration and issuing title deeds to tribals as per Land Transfer Regulation (LTR) Act should be implemented immediately in all these areas. This issue has to be immediately addressed, since only land situated in those villages that fall within the Scheduled Areas enjoy the protection under the LTR Act 1/70 in Andhra Pradesh.

The Agency Revenue Divisional Officers serve as judicial magistrates and conduct agency courts in the Scheduled Areas. They are not knowledgeable of judicial matters and LTR, as they are posted from the Revenue Department. Because of their inexperience, numerous land alienation cases are pending in such courts. Some such SDCs are given charge of more than one district, or have to deal with both plain areas and scheduled areas, causing all sorts of logistical and experiential problems. They need to be trained in their LTR and judicial roles effectively. The revenue authorities (SDCs) are not restoring lands back to tribals even after High Court issued orders.

The implementation of the LTR Act seems to be restricted to small non-tribal land holdings, while the big landlords with huge tracts of tribal land remain unaffected. Lands are being taken over by non-tribal; while the tribals have no access to their ancestral lands. In fact, The Endowments department has plans to auction such lands to private bidders. These developments are in contravention of the Fifth Schedule and the LTR Act and therefore such moves should be withdrawn forthwith. Non-tribals are using Court stay orders, and even acknowledgements from the High Court to halt the restoration of lands in LTR cases. Steps need to be taken to ensure that stay orders do not stall the restoration process. One possibility would be to enshrine the LTR Act under the IX Schedule of the Constitution.

Non-tribals are taking possession of lands in Scheduled Areas by marrying tribal women. Most often, the tribal women, who are legal owners of lands and yields, become concubines and are denied all enjoyment over such rights by the non-tribal men. The children of a non-tribal father should not be given tribal status as most of the tribal groups in the country follow a patriarchal system of identity and ownership over property. It was felt that this system should be followed in the tribal area as well in order to prevent land alienation. Section 3(1) of LTR Act should be accordingly amended prohibiting transfer of land to children of tribal women married to non-tribal men. Land alienation within tribes is a serious problem.

A special protection should be provided for the local tribes by a process of categorization of tribes both for the purpose of preventing land alienation from lesser-developed tribes, and for a more equal distribution of reservations and other constitutional provisions. As commons are difficult to manage, tribal people have frequently been denied from their rights over land. Their compulsion leads to a situation where tribals purchased seeds and other components from local money lenders in loan which ultimately displaced them from their lands due to chronic indebtedness. The unsatisfactory state of land records contributed a lot to the problem of land alienation. The tribals were never legally recognized as owners of the lands which they cultivated. The second form of land alienation is reported to have taken place due to 'benami' transfers. Another form of land alienation is related to the leasing or mortgaging of the land. To raise loans for various needs the tribals have to give their land as mortgage to the local moneylenders or to the rich farmers. Encroachment is another form of dispossessing the tribals of their lands and this is done by the new entrants in all the places where there were no proper land records.

Bribing the local Patwari for manipulating the date of settlement of land disputes, ante-dating etc., are resorted to claim the tribal lands. However, being the natural owners of forests and its adjoining lands the tribals are being deprived of their rights to own them. They have been relegated from their earlier 'self-reliant' status to a 'dependent' one. Coupled with the exploitation by the non-tribal, the State legislations also proved detrimental to their interests. Therefore to understand the root causes of the land alienation process of the tribal communities its relationship with the changes in the socio- economic structures have to be understood properly. Strong tribal movements and protests have resulted is Supreme Court's decision of forming 6th schedule and 5th schedule to protect tribal people from outsider's exploitation. Analysis of forest policies show historically forest has been seen as a commodity. It was a view primarily related to colonial administrators. In post-colonial period forest is continued to be viewed as a commodity but there was substantive concern for forest protection. This protection initiative ultimately resulted in forest protection at the expense of tribal rights. Indian tribes have historical connection with forest. They are functionally and emotionally attached to the forest. Functionally they collect Food, Fuel and Fodder three most vital ingredient of their daily life.

The Forest Charter, 1855 first time put restriction on the exploitation of forest by tribal people. Subsequently acts of 1878, 1898, 1927 and 1935 have systematically reduced tribal access to and command over forest. While tribes gradually lose their access increasing commercial exploitation increased. After independence, the nature of the acts remained largely the same until 2006. When the demands of modern industries situated outside the tribal areas led to the commercial exploitation of forests. These then became an important source of revenue in the state, and to regulate the extraction of timber and other produce, large forest areas were designated as "reserved" and put under the control of a government department. Tribal communities dwelling in enclaves inside the forest were either evicted or denied access to the forest produce on which they had depended for many necessities. Thus arose a conflict between the traditional tribal ownership and the state's claim to the entire forest wealth. Numerous revolts were the direct result of the denial of the local tribal right in the forests which they had always considered their communal property.

While they were forbidden to take even enough wood to build their huts or fashion their ploughs, they saw contractors from the lowlands felling hundreds of trees and carting them off, usually with the help of labor brought in from outside. Where tribals were allowed access to some of the forest produce, such as grass or dead wood for fuel, this was considered a "concession" liable to be withdrawn at any time. The traditional de facto ownership of tribal communities was now replaced by the de jure ownership of the state, which ultimately led to the exploitation of forest resources with total disregard for the needs of the tribal economy.

However, in 2006 India reasserted tribal's access and rights over forest land on which they have depended for centuries. Landlessness has been arguably the major cause of indebtedness among the agriculturist tribals. In India 58% of the tribal people are Below Poverty Line (BPL) with a high concentration in states like Andhra, Rajasthan, UP, Bihar, Orissa and West Bengal. The land alienation with its long history has natural consequence of indebtedness, which further lead to dispossession of tribal land. The poverty, land alienation indebtedness and landlessness are working a cyclical way. Economically indebtedness is an outcome of deficit family income and social compulsions. Since ethnographic study has shown the self-contained tribal life among the hunters and gatherers and their lack of concept of loan and interest, it is reasonable to believe that indebtedness is an outcome of interaction between non-tribal and tribal people. The tribal lack of education and understanding of loan and interests have provided the incentives to the non tribals to systematically exploit them.

2. **Bonded Labor:** Slavery convention (1926) and International Labor Organization (ILO) (1930) argue forced labor, bonded labor is to be defined on the basis of labor and services extracted from a person as a penalty where the person has not involved voluntarily. United Nations sees characteristically more complex. Major reasons of bonded labor are– Link between caste, social structure and bondage, traditional feudal social relations and bonded labor. Small scale and localized quarrying and mining invite laborers from nomadic tribes and rural poor. They are irregularly paid and are made bonded without proper work place protection. Instances are reported from Haryana, U.P, M.P, Rajasthan, Karnataka and Tamil Nadu. India has a strong and substantive bonded labor abolition act of 1976. It recognizes:

   a. overlap between forced and bonded labor,

   b. contract labor and interstate migration issues,

c. embeddedness within social customs.

However, since states showed reluctance and it is challenging to identify bonded labors, Supreme Court has tasked National Human Rights Commission for monitoring the implementation of the act.

3. **Issues Related to Health**: Malnutrition, as expected, is the most common health problem among tribal. In addition, communicable diseases such as tuberculosis, malaria, and STDs are major public health problems. Some tribal groups are also at high risk for sickle cell anemia. Generally tribal diets are seen to be deficient in protein, iron, iodine, and vitamins. According to the NFHS survey 47%, of tribal women are having chronic energy deficiency (CED) compared to 35% among the general population. The most common diseases seen among tribals are respiratory tract infections and diarrheal disorders. 21% of children suffer at least two bouts of diarrhea every year and 22% suffer from at least two attacks of respiratory infections. Tribals account for 25% of all malaria cases occurring in India and 15% of all falciparum cases. Intestinal helminthiasis is widely prevalent among tribal children (up to 50% in Orissa and 75% in MP). Skin infections such as tinea and scabies are seen among tribals due to poor personal hygiene. Sexually transmitted diseases are relatively more common (7.2% prevalence of syphilis among Kolli hills tribal's of Tamil Nadu). The prevalence of tuberculosis is high, especially in Orissa. Sickle cell trait prevalence varies from 0.5% to 45%, disease prevalence is around 10%. It is mostly seen among the tribals of central and southern India, not reported in North-East.

The prevalence of tobacco use is 44.9% among tribal men and 24% among tribal women. Tribal people from their basic ways of living remote places and shyness of mixing with community at large frequently are worst sufferers of health hazards. The per capita health expenditure among tribal is higher than regular population. The available health infrastructure, i.e. number of health care centers, professionals, and distance is considered to be determinants of the quality of health care facilities available. However, many recent studies have shown that sometimes; even if, health care facilities are available tribal tend to depend on their traditional system. The World Health Report (2000), therefore have stressed on the importance of health delivery in health outcomes, also stressing on the awareness generation about hygiene and available health infrastructure. The role of indirect intervention where removal of chronic poverty and a culture change was thought to be the prime factor for improvement of health and hygiene. At the time of independence the Government system of health care was wholly urban centered. The rural areas depended on traditional faith healers and voluntary agencies especially those of missionaries. The importance of making health service facilities available at micro level with more emphasis on tribals cannot be undermined. As a result the health issues are dealt by clubbing them together with nutrition, sanitation, family planning, health education, awareness generation etc. The village community health workers chosen by village people it now follows a decentralized agenda.

4. **Problem of Illiteracy:** The rate of illiteracy among the Scheduled Tribes has been very high. Almost 90 per cent of the tribal people were illiterates in 1961.The literacy level range from 8.5 per cent to 16, 3 per cent among the Scheduled Tribes during 1961-1981. The levels of literacy among females rose from 3.2 per cent to 8.04 per cent during the last decade. Education helps all-round developments of mind, body, culture and ultimately leads to the welfare of individual and society, through with people can enjoy the economic fruits of their efforts.

Economic development of a nation always depends on education. If people are illiterate, the concerned authorities cannot implement strict economic policies and programs. Prior to 1950, the Government of India had no direct programme for the education of tribal people. With the adoption of the constitution, the promotion of Scheduled Tribes has become a special responsibility of both the Central and State Governments. Educational opportunities have not been equal for all, especially the tribals. Most of the tribal children out of the race under severe handicaps owing to circumstances of family, peer group or social environment. For a tribal family, to send it's grown up girl or boy to school is essentially a matter of economics, and entails dislocation in the traditional pattern of division of labor. Many parents cannot just afford to send their children to school. Lack of education is a stumbling block to the tribals in attaining a higher standard of life. Though some of the tribal settlements have elementary schools within short distances and though education is free, many tribals refrain from sending their children to schools due to many reasons-1, Loss of good chunk of their labor force, 2. The fear of expenditure on education and 3. The problem of motivating the children to take their studies seriously is the most important amongst them (Jacob John Kaltaka, 1983).

5. **Problem of shifting Cultivation:** Shifting cultivation is a practice prevalent throughout the world, particularly in hill areas, inhabited by tribals. In shifting cultivation, cultivators do not stick to a particular piece of land for cultivation. A patch of land is selected; all the shrubs herbs and trees are cut down and then set on fire. The clearings thus obtained are taken up for cultivation. This type of tillage known to anthropologists as slash and burn, or Swidden cultivation. Shifting cultivation which is known by different names; Jhum in Assam and Tripura, Bewar or Oahiya in Madhya Pradesh, Koman or Bringu in north Orissa; Gudia in south Orissa and Podu in Andhra Pradesh. It has been estimated by some scientists that about 2.6 million tribal people live in the interior hilly areas, practice shifting cultivation in India. About 1.35 million acres of land, in the states of Andhra Pradesh, Arunachal Pradesh, Assam, Meghalaya, Mizoram, Manipur, Madhya Pradesh, Nagaland, Tripura, Bihar, Orissa, Kerala and Karnataka is affected. Several tribes of Andhra Pradesh were traditionally podu cultivators. In the districts of Srikakulam, Visakapatnam, Khammam, Vest Godavari and East Godavari shifting cultivation is still the main method of tillage of a number of tribal communities and is carried on side by side with plough cultivation, wherever tribals are in a state of transition between the two systems. In East Godavari District, the areas under 'podu' are far larger, and mainly in the hills of Rampachodavaram mandal. Restrictions imposed by forest officials are here not very rigorous.

6. **Economic Status:** Tribal government programmes have not significantly helped the tribals in raising their economic status. The British policy had led to ruthless exploitation of the tribals in various ways as it favored the zamindars, landlords, moneylenders, forest contractors, and excise, revenue and police officials.

7. **Banking Facility:** Banking facilities in the tribal areas are so inadequate that the tribals have to depend mainly on moneylenders. Being miserably bogged down in indebtedness, tribals demand that Agricultural Indebtedness Relief Acts should be enacted so that they may get back their mortgaged land.

8. **Crimes against Tribal Population:** India is committed to the welfare and development of its people in general and of vulnerable sections of society in particular. Equality of status and opportunity to all citizens of the country is guaranteed by the Constitution of India, which also provides that no individual shall be discriminated against on the grounds of religion, caste or sex, etc. Fundamental Rights and other specific provisions, namely, Articles 38, 39 and 46 in the Constitution of India stand testimony to the commitment of the State towards its people. The strategy of the State is to secure distributive justice and allocation of resources to support programmes for social, economic and educational advancement of the weaker sections in general and those of Scheduled Castes and Scheduled Tribes in particular. The Scheduled Tribes in India, constituting almost 8.6% of the total population, have not remained untouched from various crimes. They have been victims of countless crimes, both because of their gullibility and lack of hearing of their grievances. Looking at the year wise comparative data on the crimes committed against Scheduled Tribes, from 2006 to 20012, it is seen that: Murders decreased from 2006 to 2010 but increased in the year 2011 and 2012.The increase in murders in 2012 was about 9.09% over the year 2011. Rapes decreased from 2006 to 2009 but increased in 2010 and 2011. However a marginal fall of 5.57% was noticed in 2012 over 2011. Similar trend was seen in case of Kidnappings and abductions with a sharp decline of 24.82% in 2012. Dacoity also registered a fall of 28.57% in 2012 over 2011 while Robbery rose significantly in 2012 over 2011 and from 2006 to 2007, Arson steadily decreased from 2008 to 2012 with an increase in 2010. The increase in Arson in 2012 was about 8.33% over the year 2011.

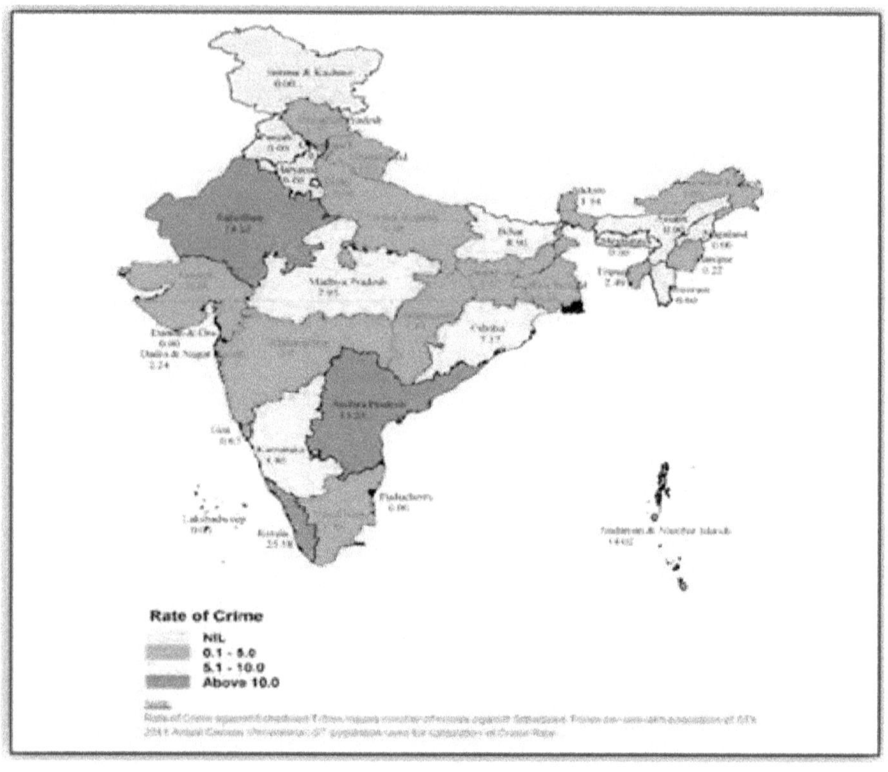

Fig 3.3: Rate of Crime against Tribes in Indian States.

SUMMARY:

The solutions to the tribal problems mentioned above, have their own merits and demerits. The modern culture must not be imposed on them. Only those elements of new culture which may vitalize them for material advancement must be infused in them. Tribal problems are simple but very delicate to handle. No solution can be experimented with before winning the confidence of the tribals. It is essential to establish a harmonious compatibility between the tribal mode of living and the material advancement of culture. The integration of the tribal society into the Indian society takes time, and it has to be promoted while retaining the good points of the tribal culture. Tribal people possess a variety of culture and they are in many ways certainly not backward. There is no point in trying to make them a second rate copy of ourselves.

We should unite and integrate the tribes in a true heart unity with India as a whole so that they may play a full part in their life. And the last is to develop welfare and educational facilities so that every tribesman may have an equal opportunity with the rest of the fellow citizens who work in the fields, factories, and workshops in the open country and the plains. The socio-cultural change among the tribal communities has no doubt empowered the tribals; however, their cultural identity is under severe stress. However, it is not too late to rise above the politics of exclusion and marginalization, to unearth and mainstream fast vanishing tribal traditions, in India. Perhaps it's time to amplify long marginalized voices and awaken contemporary Nation States to the realization that only through the establishment of such democratic, reconciliatory, gender friendly grass root tribal traditions could one create a more equitable, more just society and world order. The reality remaining that without rapid action, these native communities may be wiped out, taking with them vast indigenous knowledge, rich culture and traditions, and any hope of preserving the natural world, and a simpler, more holistic way of life for future generations. However, it will only work, if the winners support with the losers.

GLOSSARY:

1. **Bards:** Singing poets who recite verses about the legends Migrant Tribes / Nomads and history of their people.
2. **Brachycephalic:** Referring to a person with a comparatively broad head. Demography : The statistical analysis and description of populations considering vital aspects like age, sex, birth rate, death rate and mobility over a period or at one time.
3. **Generic:** Relating to or descriptive of an entire group or class.
4. **People of India Project:** The People of India Project launched by the Anthropological Survey of India in 1985 to present a brief but descriptive anthropological profile of all the communities of India, study the impact of change and development processes on these communities.

CHECK YOUR PROGRESS:

1. The progress in tribal areas of India has been a mixed bag, with some regions witnessing significant improvements in recent years.
2. One of the key problems faced by tribal communities in India is land alienation, as their traditional lands are often taken away for various development projects.
3. Lack of access to quality education and healthcare facilities remains a pressing issue in many tribal areas, hindering their socio-economic development.
4. Unemployment and underemployment are common challenges, as tribal communities often lack the necessary skills for modern job markets.
5. Tribal populations often struggle to preserve their cultural heritage and traditions in the face of rapid urbanization and globalization.
6. Government initiatives like the PESA Act (Panchayats Extension to Scheduled Areas Act) aim to empower tribal communities by granting them greater control over local governance.
7. Efforts to improve infrastructure, such as road connectivity and electrification, have been made in some tribal areas to bridge the development gap.

REFERENCES:

1. Ahmad, A. (1999): Social Geography, Rawat Publications, New Delhi, pp. 122.

2. Banerjee, Maya (1976): Tribal Population of Singhbum, Geographical Review of India, Vol. 38, No.2, June, pp.179-186.
3. Census of India, District Census Handbook Dhule and Nandurbar Districts 1981,1991 and 2001
4. Chandana, R. C and Sidhu, M. S (1980): Introduction to Population Geography, Kalyani Publishers, New Delhi, pp. 203.

5. Chib, S. S. (1981): Tribal Population of India: A Geographical Interpretation, The National Geographical Journal of India, Vol. 27, Parts 3 & 4, Sept- Dec, pp 128-136.

6. Clarke, John (1972): "Population Geography", Pergamon Press, Oxford.

7. Gosal, G. S. (1982): Recent Population Growth in India, Population Geographer, Vol. 4 pp33- 53.

8. Hornby, W. F and Jones, W. (1980): An Introduction to Population Geography, Cambridge University, Press, Cambridge, p.20.

9. Muzumdar, K. (1973) Distribution of Tribal Population in Eastern Gujarat, The National Geographical Journal of India, Vol. XIV (Parts 3& 4) pp 177.

10. Nagada, B. L (2001): Tribal Population and Health in Rajasthan, Studies of Tribes and Tribals", Kamal Raj Enterprises, New Delhi, Vol 2, No. 1 pp. 1-8.

11. Patil, V. B (1998): An Introduction to Tribal Culture and Tribals in Maharashtra, (ed), Tribal Research Bulletin. (Developmental 59 Scheme Special Issue), Tribal Research and Training Institute, Pune, Vol. XX No.1 Mar. 1998. pp. 1-6.

12. Ramesh, C. R (1965): Population Trends in the Malad, The Deccan Geographers, Vol. III, NO.1, p.67.

13. Ramotra, K. C and Mote, Y. S. (2009) Growth and Distribution of Tribal Population in Dhule and Nandurbar Districts of Maharashtra: A Geographical Analysis. Tribal Research Bulletin, Tribal Research and Training Institute, Pune Vol. XXXIII No. 1, pp 15- 24.

14. Ramotra, K. C. (2008): Development Processes and the Scheduled Castes, Rawat Publications, Jaipur.

15. Raza, Moonis and Aijazuddin Ahmad (1990). "An Atlas of Tribal India" Concept Publishing Company A/15-16 Commercial Block, Mohan Garden, New Delhi – 110059.

16. Sanyal, S. (1980): Some Demographic Aspects of the Scheduled Tribes of Andaman and Nicobar Islands, Man in India, Vol. LX. No. 34, pp.204-220.

17. Singh, R. N and Chaturvedi, R. B (1983): Dynamics of Population in Bundelkhand Region: A case Study, Journal of Association of Population Geographer.

18. Virginius,2003. Tribes in India in The Oxford India Companion to Sociology and Social Anthropology Edited by Veena Das; Oxford University Press: New Delhi.

19. Vidyarthi, L.P. and B.K. Rai. 1977. The Tribal Culture of India. Delhi: Concept Publishing Company

TERMINAL QUESTIONS:

A. **Long Questions**

1. Define tribe and explain its classification with suitable illustration.

2. What do you understand by tribes? Differentiate between tribes of north east and western India

3. Explain spatial distribution of Tribes in India

4. How the tribal population in India changing spatially and temporally, Evaluate.

5. What are the problems faced by tribes in India, describe.

B. **Short questions**

1. What are tribal areas, and how are they distinct from other regions?
2. What are the major challenges faced by tribal communities?
3. How does lack of access to healthcare impact tribal populations?
4. What are the economic challenges commonly experienced by tribal people?
5. Write a short note on the distribution of tribal population in India.
6. How does cultural preservation and identity relate to tribal issues?
7. What is the impact of inadequate infrastructure in tribal regions?
8. Write a short note on the tribes of India.
9. What is status of banking facility in tribal area and how this is impacting their development?
10. What efforts can be made to address the problems faced by tribal populations?

C. **Multiple choice questions**

1. What are tribal areas primarily known for?

    A. Industrial development
    B. Urbanization
    C. Traditional and rural livelihoods
    D. Education and technology (Answer: C)

2. Which of the following is a common issue faced by tribal children in terms of education?

    A. Access to quality schools
    B. Overwhelming technological resources
    C. Abundant learning materials
    D. High literacy rates (Answer: A)

3. Land rights and ownership are significant issues in tribal areas because:

    A. Land is abundant and easily accessible
    B. Tribes typically don't use land for agriculture
    C. Land is a crucial source of livelihood and identity
    D. Land is not important in tribal culture (Answer: C)

4. Inadequate healthcare infrastructure in tribal areas can lead to:

    A. High life expectancy
    B. Improved overall health outcomes
    C. Health disparities and increased mortality rates
    D. Equal access to healthcare services (Answer: C)

5. What is an important aspect of tribal culture that needs preservation and support?

    A. Assimilation into mainstream culture
    B. Loss of traditional languages and customs
    C. Urbanization and modernization
    D. Access to modern technology (Answer: B)

6. Which of the following is a common economic issue in tribal areas?

   A. High income levels
   B. Low poverty rates
   C. Economic disparities and poverty
   D. Abundant job opportunities (Answer: C)

7. What role does government policy play in the development of tribal communities?

   A. No significant role
   B. Hindrance to progress
   C. Can either promote or hinder development
   D. Solely responsible for development (Answer: C)

8. Environmental concerns in tribal areas often revolve around:

   A. Limited access to natural resources
   B. Overexploitation of resources
   C. Lack of interest in environmental issues
   D. Abundance of pristine ecosystems (Answer: B)

9. How can tribal people be empowered in decision-making processes?

   A. Through exclusion from decision-making
   B. By prioritizing their input and participation
   C. By imposing decisions from outside authorities
   D. By discouraging their involvement in governance (Answer: B)

10. What is the primary goal of addressing tribal area problems?

   A. Cultural assimilation
   B. Preservation of traditional practices
   C. Ensuring sustainable development and well-being
   D. Ignoring their unique needs (Answer: C)

CHAPTER FOUR

POPULATION PROBLEMS AND POLICIES

INTRODUCTION

The term Population has been defined differently in different contexts. For social science the population can be defined as 'total number of people of a particular group, race, class, category (e.g. Population of Scheduled Castes, Scheduled Tribes, or religious groups) or of a specified area or territory (e.g. Population of world, country, state, city or village).

Population is a great human resource which paves way for technological, socio-economic and cultural development in a society. But its excess is a great curse which produces a wide variety of impediments to development and creates a number of problems. The genesis of the population lies in the excessive growth and over population. If the growth of population exceeds the optimum size of the population nourished by the economic and technological development of the region, it creates over population which is a universal problem in all developing countries of the world.

Over population puts heavy pressure on existing factor endowments, especially natural resources of the community. This leads to resources depletion and crisis leading to economic retardation and deprivation. This also causes poor quality of life, low standards of living, mass poverty, disease and hunger. Similarly shortage of food, inadequate housing, lack of health care, mother care and family welfare facilities, illiteracy, unemployment, insanitation price rise, adulteration, hoarding, black marketing, theft, loot, strikes, lockouts, environmental pollution, political upheaval etc. are all related to explosive and uncontrolled population growth.

Every nook and corner of India is a clear display of increasing population. Whether you are in a metro station, airport, railway station, road, highway, bus stop, hospital, shopping mall, market, temple, or even in a social/ religious gathering, we see all these places are overcrowded at any time of the day. This is a clear indication of overpopulation in the country. According to the Indian census, carried out in 2011, the population of India was exactly 1,210,193,422, which means India has crossed the 1-billion mark. In spite of the fact that the population policies, family planning and welfare programmes undertaken by the Govt. of India, have led to a continuous decrease in the fertility rate, yet the actual stabilization of population can take place only by 2050.

POPULATION PROBLEMS AND POLICIES

CONCEPT OF UNDER, OVER AND OPTIMUM POPULATION:

1. Under Population:

If the population of a country is below the optimum, i.e., below what it ought to be, then the country is said to be under-populated. Further, it can be stated that when the number of the people are insufficient to take the fullest possible advantage of the natural and capital resources of the country, the region can be called as under populated. In other words, under population occurs when a population is too small to utilize its available resources, or where resources could support a larger population with no reduction in living standards. Examples of under population are found in certain regions of low development such as areas of subsistence agriculture and pastoral nomadism etc. Under population is a situation whereby the size of the population is small in relation to available resources of the country. It is situation where the size of the population is below the equilibrium

Causes of under population:

1. **An increase in Death Rate:** Natural Catastrophes such as earthquakes, flood etc. will lead to an increase in death rate therefore the country

witnesses a reduction

2. **A fall in Birth Rate:** When a country decides to reduce the number of children for fear of eventual overpopulation or any socio-political factor which does not favor children, the country becomes under-populated
3. **High Level of Emigration:** A persistent increase in migration will leads to a reduction in a country population.

Positive effects of under population

1. No Congestion: A country with less population experiences little or no congestion.
2. Employment Opportunities: As a result of small size of the population, there will be enough job opportunity for the people.
3. Increased in Social and Infrastructural Facilities: An under Populated Country experiences a higher per capita in terms of social and infrastructural facilities available to the people in the country.
4. Availability of Idle Resources: The fact that a country is less populated means that the resource available in that country is higher than the number of people; hence, many idle resources would abound everywhere.

Negative Effects of under population

1. Lower Standard of Living: Under Population engender lower standard of living as a result of inadequate labor force that would have conveniently boost output and production of goods and services.
2. Lack of Adequate Manpower: Under population results to shortage of labor with that attendant effect of low investments and income.
3. Underutilization of Resources: Resources are highly underutilized in a country with low population.
4. Lack of People to Defend the Country: At times of war and emergency, a country might find it difficult to mobilize enough people to defend it.
5. Equilibrium at Less than Full Employment: Under population leads to reaching of equilibrium at less than full employment as a result of idle resources.

2. Over Population:

Any area is over populated when the carrying capacity of an area is exceeded by its population. It means the area has more population than what it can support. Over population exists where there is an excess of population over utilized or potential resources. It may result from an increase in population or a decline in resources. Therefore, it means, over population occurs when resource development fails to keep pace with population growth. As there is no measurement of over population, it is simply characterized with low per capita income, high population density, low living standards, higher unemployment and outmigration. In extreme condition, the symptoms of over population are famine, poverty, hunger, malnutrition etc.

3. Optimum Population:

Optimum population has been defined in several ways by different people. Cloud (1971) defined "optimum population as the one that lies within limits, large enough to realize the potentials of human creativity to achieve a life of high quality for all the inhabitants indefinitely, but not so large as to threaten dilution of quality or the potential to achieve it or the wise management of the ecosystem". Knowles and Wareing (2011) have defined optimum population as 'the size of population enabling maximum per capita output and the highest possible living standards under given economic and technological conditions'(Fig. 4.1).

Another definition says that by optimum population is meant the ideal number of the population that a country should have, considering its resources. The optimum means the best and the most desirable size of a country's population consistent with its resources. It is the right number. When a country's population is neither too big nor too small, but just that much which the country ought to have, it is called the optimum population. Therefore, it is clear that given a certain amount of resources, state of technical knowledge and a certain stock of capital, there will be a definite size of the population at which real income of goods and services per capita will be the highest. This is the optimum size. The optimum number can, therefore, be defined as the one at which per capita income is the highest. Optimum population also refers to the size of a population that produces the best results according to chosen targets.

In present context, it can be defined as that size of population which the earth's carrying capacity can support and shall ensure the highest level of sustainable development in a region. The level of sustainable development here means that the relationship between man-nature is highly developed not at the cost of each other but in relation to each other. At present many countries are experiencing manmade problems due to the disregard of environment. For example flood is no more a natural disaster, pollution etc. These problems are limiting the rapid economic development of a region. In tackling these anthropogenic problems, the pace of economic development gets hampered. Therefore, optimum population is one which makes a region more comfortable with respect to maximum resource development plus the suitable environment for the living conditions of the local.

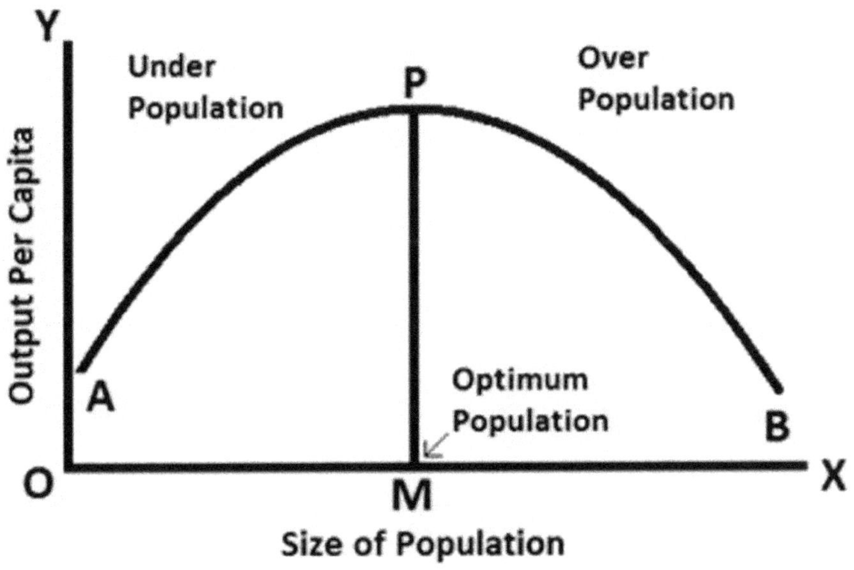

Fig. 4.1: Under, optimum and over population.

RELATIONSHIP BETWEEN UNDER, OVER AND OPTIMUM POPULATION

The resources are vast; much can be produced; but there are not men enough to carry on the work of production efficiently (state of under population). Under such conditions, increase in population will be followed by an increase in the per capita income. But this increase cannot go on indefinitely. When the shortage of man-power has been made up, the per capita income will reach the maximum, and we shall say that the optimum has been reached. If, the population still goes on increasing and the optimum is exceeded, then we shall have a state of over population. There will be too many people on the land. The resources will not be sufficient to provide gainful employment to all. They will be thinly spread over the teeming millions. Per capita income will diminish; the standard of living will fall; war, famine and disease will be constant companions of such a people in the region.

It is generally agreed that a small manageable increase in population is not objectionable in an expanding economy. However, it is clear that beyond a certain level, population increase may become excessive, so that the economy gets exhausted and problems associated with over population such as poverty, malnutrition and starvation reach serious proportions. The problem lies in assessing when the optimum population for any given economy has been reached, or the point when population growth becomes excessive. Although, the determination of optimum population is difficult, it nevertheless seems clear that most of the developing countries have already passed this point.

POPULATION PROBLEMS:

India is one of the more densely populated countries of the world. It has to support about 15% of the world population, although its land area is merely 2.4% of the land area of the world. India's population stood at 1027,015,247 on March 1, 2001. The decennial census of 2001 indicates an addition of 181 million people between 1991 and 2001 but the rate of growth in this decade shows the sharpest decline (21.34%) since independence.

The exponential rate of growth of population (annual) in the decades 1991-2001 was 1.9% as against 2.1% the previous decade. But it was still higher than the assumptions regarding from 1.6 to 1.8% made by the planning commission.

The rate of population growth depends on the difference between the birth rate and the death rate. Thus, the population growth experienced in India can largely be explained by variations in birth and death rates.

The death rate continued to fall over the entire plan period. But the birth rate continues to remain high by current standards. As a result there has been a net addition to the size of the population.

A study of India's demographic trends during the last five decades reveals that the death rate has fallen much faster than the birth rate. The death rate has already fallen to a very low level (viz., 9.6 per thousand). There is no scope for reducing it further. But the birth rate continues to be high by current standards. Therefore, in future India's population will be a function of birth rate alone.

The Nature of India's Population Problem:

The number of people which a country can support largely, if not entirely, depends upon its existing natural resources, the methods it uses in production, and the efficiency of labor which affects labor productivity. This problem is becoming more and more acute day by day due to rapidly increasing population— by about 22 million persons a year. So, India is over-populated.

However, a small minority of people see that India is not really over-populated because it is a vast country with plenty of natural resources. These resources have not been fully used as yet. They express the view that, if all the resources are fully employed, India can maintain a larger population than what it is having now and in much greater comfort. There is some truth in this argument. But one cannot deny the following facts:

1. The population of India is very large by current standards.
2. The rate of increase of population is also high i.e. about 2.22% per year, in absolute form this comes to nearly 22 million persons per annum.
3. Even the existing population is not being fed, clothed and housed properly; most people are living in miserable conditions.
4. The modest increase in national income under planned economic development is being eaten up by the increase in population. As a result, the per capita income growth has almost reached a vanishing point.
5. The need of controlling population is urgent and pressing so that the existing people may have an improved standard of living.
6. There is no denying of the fact that there are too many people now in India. However, the real problem is not the present large size of the population but the rate at which the size of population is increasing every year. India can progress, if and only if, the continuous and huge increase in population is held in check.

Therefore, the major population problem can be described in following heads:

1. **Poverty:** Poverty is a greatest problem faced by developing countries like India. Roughly 302 million of our people, or 1 in 4, live below the poverty line. The data by National Sample Survey Organization (NSSO) are based on uniform recall period consumption i.e. per capita monthly consumption expenditure (Rural Rs. 356.30; Urban Rs. 538.60). Although there is percentage decline of people below the poverty line both in rural and urban areas. Still India has the highest poverty rate amongst major countries of the world.

   Figure represents the state wise incidence of urban poverty. The distribution shows variation in poverty in different parts of the country. The lowest poverty, 5.4 percent, is recorded in Jammu and Kashmir while Orissa is characterized by the highest percentage of poverty (46.4). In Orissa, Bihar, Chhattisgarh, and Jharkhand more than 40 percent of the people live below poverty line. Uttar Pradesh, with 32.8% of population below poverty line, has the largest number of poor (59 million) in India. On the other hand southern states have lower poverty (20-30 percent). Lowest poverty can be seen in the western and northern states of the country.

2. **Malnutrition:** There is a shortage of nourishment especially that of balanced diet in developing county like India. The standard of living is very low and housing conditions are often poor. The standard of living of hygiene and quality of nutrition are also often poor, which leads to many deficiency diseases. According to the Survey conducted by the National Sample Survey Organization in 2014-15, there has been decline in per capita intake of calories and protein between 1972-73 and 2004-05. A significant rise in per capita daily intake of fat is observed both in rural and urban areas during the same period. Since these data are at household level and do not reflect the dietary intake of the individual, especially women and children.

   Among the factors influencing malnutrition may be made of:
   (a) physical environment,
   (b) demographic variable,
   (c) socio-cultural factor, and

(d) economic variable.

Physical environment affects the crop variety, dietary habit and occurrence of diseases. Demographic variables affect the quantity and quality of the food. For example, swamp, dense vegetation, heavy rainfall and excessive irrigated areas promote the origin of vectored diseases like Malaria and Filaria etc. Iodine deficiency in the mountainous and sub-mountainous regions enhances the incidence of endemic goiter in these areas. Seasonal changes also have role in the incidence of diseases. In general summer and rainy season promote the occurrence of diseases. The size of the family and spacing in the birth of children affects the per capita availability of food. In India poor and economically depressed household are generally larger in size and low spacing in the child birth.

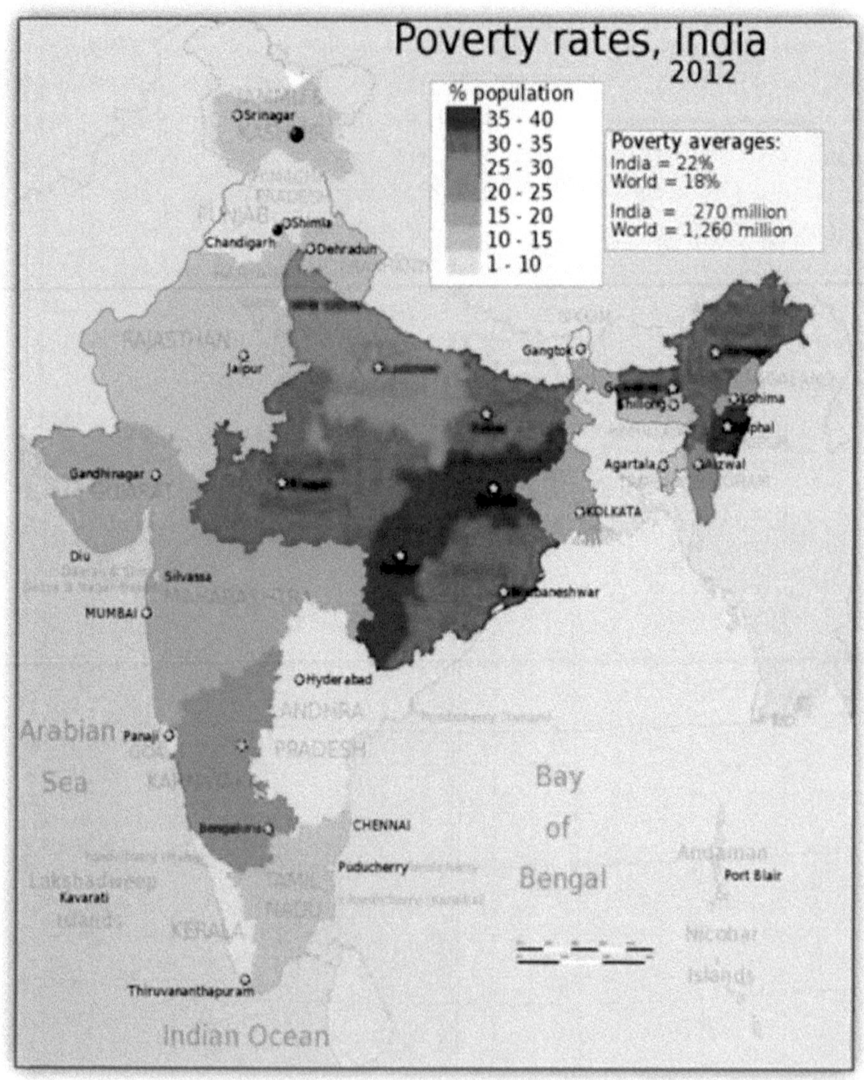

Fig.4.2 Spatial Pattern of Poverty Rates in India

In most of the states, the calories intake is higher in rural areas than urban areas, although the gap is not very large. However in the southern, central and eastern parts of the country urban areas consume more calories. In general the calories intake appears to decrease southwards and eastward into warmer region of the country.

Food security is also one another side of the problem faced by Indian population. Food security refers to the availability of food and one's access to it. Food security exists when people, at all times, have physical and economic access to sufficient, safe and nutritious food to meet their dietary needs and food preferences for an active and healthy life.

It is based on two factors; (a) food availability and (b) purchasing power of the people.

Worldwide around 852 million people are chronically hungry due to extreme poverty, while up to 2 billion people lack food security intermittently due to varying degree of poverty. In India alone despite sufficient buffer stock of food grains, an estimated 200 million people are underfed and 50 million on the brink of starvation, resulting in starvation deaths. States like Bihar, Orissa, Madhya Pradesh, Chhattisgarh and Jharkhand show low levels of food security. Gujarat and Rajasthan, which have moderately food secure population in urban areas, exhibit severe insecurity in rural areas.

3. **Migration:** The term migration refers to the movement of population from one place to another. It may be of temporary or permanent. Temporary migration may be annual, seasonal or even of a shorter duration, like daily. Migration is not merely a relocation of human resources but it is a process which has three-fold impact: (a) on the area experiencing in-migration, (b) on the area experiencing out-migration, and (c) on the migrants themselves. The purpose of migration may be employment, business, education, family movement, marriage, calamity etc. According to 2011 Census, about 40 percent of migration is due to economic reasons, especially for seeking employment.

In India there is massive rural to urban migration towards metropolitan cities like Kolkata, Mumbai, Delhi, Chennai, Hyderabad etc. to seek employment, better economic prospects and education. Majority of these migrants are illiterates and semi-literates and un- skilled, who are compelled to leave their village home due to poverty and unemployment. Since, most of our cities have very limited employment generating capacity under capital-intensive industrialization and very limited absorptive capacity in the organized sector, these migrants find salvage only in informal sector, such as porters, domestic servants, hawkers, vendors, construction workers etc.

Mukherji has termed this phenomenon of urban growth as 'involuntary urbanization'. It has led to the cancerous growth of shanty towns, slums, bastes and squatter settlements, overflow of urban employment, digression of per capita consumption levels of daily necessities very sharp decline of basic human values in extremely congested Indian metropolitan that have been speedily occurring over 1981 and which will accelerate in near future. Because of this unchecked influx India's mega cities and metropolitan are growing as a over blown villages, without essential urban function characteristics, urban infrastructure and services and without a strong economic base. The phenomenon is similar to urban decay and degeneration.

Dependency Ratio: Dependency ratio denoted the number of dependents over the working-age population. It is of three types: (a) youth dependency ratio, (b) aged dependency ratio and (c) total dependency ratio. Table shows the changes in dependency ratio in India between 1950-2005. According to the table the total dependency ratio has shown rising trends upto 1970 but it is steadily declining onwards. This is due to sharp decline in youth dependency ratio between 1970-2005, although aged dependency ratio has shown rising trends.

Year	Youth	Aged	Total
1950	0.67	0.06	0.73
1960	0.70	0.06	0.76
1970	0.72	0.07	0.79
1980	0.67	0.07	0.74
1990	0.62	0.07	0.69
2000	0.56	0.08	0.64
2005	0.52	0.08	0.60
2011	0.48	0.09	0.60

Table 4.3: India: Dependency Ration.*Source: Office of Registrar General, India*

At state level highest dependency ratio (0.95) is found in Bihar followed by Uttar Pradesh (0.93), Meghalaya (0.88), Rajasthan (0.88), Madhya Pradesh (0.84) and Jharkhand (0.84). on the other hand Daman and Diu (0.48) and Goa (0.49) have the lowest dependency ratio. Young dependency ratio almost follows the same pattern with the highest and the lowest values recorded in Bihar (0.82) and Daman and Diu (0.40) respectively. In the old dependency ratio Kerala top the list while Dadra and Nagar Haveli is in the bottom.

5. **Mismanagement of Agricultural Resources:** By and large, most of the developing countries like India have agrarian economy. The agriculture is mostly done by traditional methods; absolute equipment's had inadequate financial resources. Owing to the lack of funds and finances, the farmers are unable to apply chemical fertilizers and other inputs in required quantities. Consequently, the production per unit is low. The fragmentation and small size of holding and land tenancy systems are also some of the serious barriers in the modernization of agriculture. In such countries, land is their ultimate asset, is thus either underutilized or miss utilized. Many of the farmers, being tradition bound, do not accept the innovations and new ideas.

6. **Orthodoxy:** As said earlier, the people in the India are traditional bound, and less exposed to the outside world. Moreover, they are religious in their attitudes who do not accept easily new ideas and modern style of life. Being religious, they generally do not observe family planning. Birth control is forbidden by the Catholic Church in India, caste restriction on occupation also help to slow down transformation of society and process of development. For the removal of such attitudes and for the eradication of blind faith and orthodoxy, large scale literacy and mass education are necessary.

7. **Population and Environment:** According to some research, environmental pollution is one of the serious problems faced by the people in the country. Rapid population growth, industrialization and urbanization in country are adversely affecting the environment. Though the relationship is complex, population size and growth tend to expand and accelerate these human impacts on the environment. All these in turn lead to an increase in the pollution levels. However, environmental pollution not only leads to deteriorating environmental conditions but also have adverse effects on the health of people. India

is one of the most degraded environment countries in the world and it is paying heavy health and economic price for it. According to the World Development Indicators report in 1997, 1.5 billion people live exposed to dangerous levels of air pollution, 1 billion live without clean water and 2 billion live without sanitation. The increase of population has been tending towards alarming situation. The world's population was estimated to be 6.14 billion in mid 2001and projected 7.82 billion and 9.04 billion in the year 2025 and 2050 respectively. Contribution of India alone to this population was estimated to be 1033 million in the mid 2001 which has been projected 1363 million and 1628 million in 2025 and 2050 respectively. (2001 World Population Data Sheet). According to the provisional results of the Census of India 2001, the population of India, on 1st March 2001, was 1027 million.

IMPLICATIONS OF GROWING POPULATION IN INDIA

Population growth and its relation to economic growth has been a matter of debate for over a century. The early Malthusian view was that population growth is likely to impede economic growth because it will put pressure on the available resources, result in reduction in per capita income and resources; this, in turn, will result in deterioration in quality of life. Contrary to the Malthusian predictions, several of the East Asian countries have been able to achieve economic prosperity and improvement in quality of life in spite of population growth. This has been attributed to the increase in productivity due to development and utilization of innovative technologies by the young educated population who formed the majority of the growing population. These countries have been able to exploit the dynamics of demographic transition to achieve economic growth by using the human resources as the engine driving the economic development. Improved employment with adequate emoluments has promoted saving and investment which in turn stimulated economic growth. Following are the adverse effects of population growth on the Indian Economy:

- Adverse effects on savings
- Unproductive investment
- Slow growth of Per Capita Income
- Underutilization of labor
- Growing pressure on land
- Adverse effect on quality of population and

- Adverse social impact

SOLVING THE POPULATION PROBLEM

One may suggest two measures for solving India's population problem. These are:

1. Birth control and
2. Accelerating the rate of growth of the economy.

The control of births seems to be the most common method of checking the growth of population. However, because of the low level of literacy and lack of general interest, family planning has not achieved much success so far.

Rapid economic development will surely answer our needs. In fact, China has achieved rapid growth in spite of population growth. People must be made to feel that their poverty is removable and they can enjoy all those things, which the higher income groups enjoy. Then only will they start working hard. Furthermore, they will adopt a small family norm, if they realize that a large number of children will definitely keep them poor and make them poorer.

But according to the theory of demographic transition in the initial stages there is a possibility for the birth rate to rise or, at least, to remain constant, but the death rate is bound to decline. If this happens, then birth control will have to go hand-in-hand with the acceleration of the rate of economic growth.

India's rapidly growing population is the most serious obstacle to her economic development. It is not possible to reduce the existing size of population. But it is, of course, possible to slowdown the rate at which population is increasing.

The overall development of the country and rise in per capita income can go a long way in reducing the rate of increase in population. But the birth rate will have to be reduced at the same time. The Government is using both the methods at present. However, India is a large country and most people who live in backward areas are illiterate and ignorant. Naturally, it will take time to make the Governments effort bear fruit.

In short, the wide variations in growth rate, literacy level and sex ratio would have to be taken into account in formulating new strategies to stabilizing India's population in the next for decades.

POPULATION POLICIES IN INDIA:

The sizes of the population, its structure, composition and growth rate as well as the migration pattern are closely influenced by the population policies. These policies range from encouragement of high fertility to varying degree of discouragement.

Concept of a population policy: The size of the population, its characteristics, spatial and rural-urban distribution, rate of growth and its determinants decide the quantum, pattern and distribution of consumption and production. It is, therefore, only natural for the state or the government to be concerned about population. Such concern is most essential for a complex democratic society seeking to eradicate poverty and ensure adequate standards of living for its people. Of course, even an authoritarian leader must consider the actual or potential supply of workers (including army personnel), the requisite equipment and the consumption needs of people. Therefore, the three determinants of population change – birth rate, death rate and migration to or from a territorial unit – have naturally received explicit or implicit attention from rulers or governments since the days of Kautilya.

A policy is defined as a statement of important goals, accompanied by a specified set of means to achieve them. A well-elaborated set of means constitutes a programme. A good policy has to be based on a sound theory linking the means with the ends, although on social issues it is often likely to involve an element of judgment about the connection between inputs and outcomes or the process.

Population Policy represents a strategy for achieving a particular pattern of population change. It would address itself both to the situations arising out of declining population as well as of fast rising population. This policy belongs to the category of policies of "Social Engineering" and for a less developed economy. It is a policy that refers to the governmental measures with reference to population change. Measures and programmes designed to contribute to the achievement of economic, social, demographic, political and other collective goals, through affecting critical demographic variables, namely, the size and growth of population, its geographic distribution (national and international) and its demographic characteristics. The important objectives of population policy are: primarily to reduce fertility and mortality and secondarily to manage redistribution of population. Since mortality is an un-deprivable characteristic of population, population policy aims at reduction of mortality through the concept of public health and the mass eradication of epidemics. It seeks to adjust population to the requirements of the economy and optimum spatial distribution of population.

The modern Family Planning includes:

(1) The proper spacing and limitation of births

(2) Advice on sterility

(3) Education for parenthood

(4) Sex education

(5) Screening for pathological conditions related to the reproductive system

(6) Genetic counseling

(7) Premarital consultation and examination

(8) Carrying out pregnancy tests

(9) Marriage counseling

(10) The preparation of couples for the arrival of their first child

(11) Providing services for unmarried mothers

(12) Teaching home economics and nutrition and

(13) Providing adoption services.

But the activities vary from country to country according to national family planning policies and objectives. Population policy aims at Planned Parenthood or non-parenthood. It should aim at reducing the population growth rate and at ensuring adequate replacement. A population policy can be nothing less than a social policy at large. It must work itself into the whole rubric of social life and inter-persuade and be inter-persuaded by all other measures of social change.

In India, the first reference to family planning matters can be traced back to 1916 when P.K. Wattal advocated family planning movement in his book, 'The Population Problem in India' and the first birth control centre in Bombay was opened by R.D. Kame in 1925. Yet, the British were reluctant in forming a population policy due to non-interference in local matters and controversy between the church and the parliament in Britain over birth control.

Even though, Gandhiji advocated self-control instead of other birth control measures however a small group of elite made suggestions to government to propagate information on birth control and its practice. India is having the distinction of being the first country to have an official Family

Planning Programme, which was initiated in 1952. During the third five year plan (1961-66), family planning was declared as "the very center of planned development". The amendment of the constitution in 1976 has made "population Control and Family Planning" a concurrent subject.

It is worth noting that China brought down the growth rate of population from 2.2% per annum during 1960's to 1.0 % per annum during 1990's by offering incentives such as increase in salary by 12.5 Per cent, priority in housing, preference in jobs, heavy taxation to the refusal of one-child norm etc. The Health Survey and Development Committee were appointed with Sri Joseph Bhore as Chairman in 1943. It came up with several suggestions like: -

(a) Contraceptives be manufactured and distributed with the help of the government,

(b) Marriage age be has to be increased,

(c) Knowledge, attitude and practices about family planning are to be improved and

(d) Person suffering from serious diseases be sterilized.

At the time of appointment of Planning Commission, suggestions were made by members of the health programmes social welfare, social sciences panel of the Planning Commission to include Family Planning in the first five year plan. Specific government measures were recommended including provision of facilities for sterilization or giving advice on contraception on medical, social and economic grounds. Research was recommended for the development of inexpensive, safe and efficacious methods of birth control suitable for all classes of people. There was strong elite who agreed with birth control but against the use of contraceptives. There were supporters of another view that if population is well organized, it is a source of power.

Five Year Plans and Population Policy:

The first five year plan recognized the population pressure in India which requires a population policy. In the first five year plan, the main appeal for family planning is based on consideration of health and welfare of the family. Public health programme included measures directed to family limitation or spacing of children which is necessary and desirable in order to secure better health for the mother and better care and upbringing of children. The reduction of birth rate to the extent necessary to stabilize the population at a level consistent with the requirement of national economy.

During the plan, the Government of India earmarked Rs. 6.5 million for the promotion of family planning.

The contraceptive methods advocated during this period were the rhythm, diaphragm, Jelly and foam tablets. The number of family planning clinics increased from 50 in 1951 to 165 in 1953. The family planning objective in the first five year plan was to obtain an accurate picture of the factors contributing to the rapid population increase in India, discover suitable techniques of family planning and advise methods by which knowledge of these techniques can be widely disseminated and make advice on family planning, an integral part of the services of government hospitals and public health agencies.

The plan also recommended the formation of a population policy committee in the Planning Commission and the Family Planning Research and Programme Committee (FPRPRC). The latter was formed on May 6, 1953 under the Chairmanship of C.K. Lakshmanan. The Committee laid emphasis on the maintenance of the health of the mother and welfare of the children a part of the family planning programme and it should be developed as an integral part of the health system. It further recommended for field studies as social attitudes and motivation affecting family planning.

In the second plan need for curbing birth rate was accepted even though the rate of population growth was recognized as an important factor in planning and development. The second plan reiterated the earlier policy to slow down the rate of population growth. An effective curb on population growth is an important condition for rapid improvement in income and levels of living. The Plan stated that an effective curb on population growth is an important condition for rapid improvement in income and standard of living. The end of the second plan, the number of clinics increased to 4,185.

The Third five year plan had an objective of stabilizing the growth of Population. The third plan stated the objective of stabilizing the growth of Population over a reasonable period as the Centre of planned development. The plan associated population with social policies like education of women, opening new employment opportunities for them and raising the age at marriage. The family planning programme should include sex and family life and advice on such other measures as may be necessary to promote the welfare of the family besides advice on birth control. The strategy of the programme has been shifted from the clinic approach to the community oriented Extension Approach.

The main components of the extended programme were: -

(1) Creation of social climate in which the need is felt by individual families and groups of people;

(2) Knowledge that a Small family norm is valuable to each individual permeating into every mind;

(3) Provision of readily accessible services, generally as part of health services especially health of mothers and children and

(4) Adoption of effective methods by all eligible couples.

At the end of Third plan period, the birth rate stood around 41 per thousand. Successful public health and curative measures had brought down the death rate to around 16.

The Fourth plan insisted on family planning programme as an essential and inevitable factor for development. The goal of the plan was to reduce the birth rate to 32 per 1,000 by the end of the fourth plan and to 25 per 1000 by 1981. The plan advocated that even far reaching social and economic programmes will not lead to a better life unless population growth is controlled. Limitation of family is an essential and inescapable ingredient of development'. On the eve of Fourth Plan, five central institutes and 43 family planning training centers were functioning. There were 4840 rural family welfare planning centers, 21,572 rural sub-centers and 1856 urban family welfare planning centers were in operation.

During the Fifth Plan period (1974-1979), the National Population Policy was announced in April 1976 with a target of reduction of birth rate of 25 per thousand, and a population growth rate of 1.4 per cent by 1980. The legal minimum age at marriage was brought up from 15 to 18 for females from 17 to 21 for males. Any violation of the law could be treated as a cognizable offense. The plan attributed the poor growth rate of the economy in the previous plan to the excessive growth rate of population. The aims of the plan were to reduce the birth rate to 30 per 1,000 by 1978-79 and to 25 per 1,000 by 1983-84.

The internal emergency was declared in the country in June 1975 and continued up to March 1977. Several target-oriented, time-bound and coercive measures were resorted to during this period. The Central Government permitted the State governments to pass legislation for the compulsory sterilization for couples with a minimum of three living children. The family planning was considered as a multi-faceted problem and the contribution of all other ministries was sought for the implementation of the problem. Several measures were maintained in the policy such as graded monetary compensations based on the number of living children at the time of sterilization. A new record was created with a reported 10 million sterilizations during this period.

The draft of Sixth Five Year Plan stated that a population policy should reflect concern for the individuals as well as the community's dignity, needs and aspirations, and should be such as would deal with overall development issues and not merely population control. The Plan document envisaged the establishment of a unified, standardized, monolithic pattern of health and family planning for the country and urged that it should be varied to meet 197 differing conditions and take regional variations into account. All the plan projections of reduction of poverty and unemployment will go wrong, if success is not achieved in curtailing the growth of population.

The Plan emphasized on demographic goals not only in terms of fertility reduction and mortality reduction and distribution of population, but also in terms of employment and standard of living. The targets put forth in the Sixth Plan are: infant mortality rate to 65 for rural and 50 for urban, maternal mortality below 2, death rate 9, birth rate 21, net reproduction rate of I by the year 2000. The plan allotted an outlay of Rs. 17,750 million for the programme. The performance under the programme during the Sixth Plan was 79.2% of Sterilizations, 81.7% of IUD users and 85.4% of C.C. users was achieved and the increase in couple protection rate was by 9.8 points.

The Seventh Plan stressed the necessity of breaking the vicious circle of adverse circumstances resulting in low contraception and high birth rates. A more comprehensive National population policy was adopted in 1986, by the Government. It was promoted on a voluntary basis as a "Movement of the people, by the people, for the people". This policy has given the family planning a broader perspective by giving importance to female literacy rate, enhance child survival through universal immunization and promotion of oral rehydration therapy, anti-poverty programmes, revamping infrastructure, promotion of two-child family norm etc., in addition to usual measures of raising age at marriage for females to 20 years, Maximum involvement was sought on the part of non-governmental institutions. The Seventh Five Year Plan stated a multi-disciplinary approach through voluntary peoples programme and to generate environment for fertility decline through relevant socio-economic intervention. The goals of family welfare were envisaged in the plan. They were to achieve CBR of 29.1 per 1000, CDR of 10.4 per 1,000, infant mortality of 90 per 1000. live births, effective couple protection rate to be increased to 42 per cent by the year 1990. New infrastructure was created in certain States.

The Eighth Plan envisaged the bringing down of the birth rate in India from 30.5 per thousand to 20 per thousand by the year 2000. It noted that the addition of about 1.8 crore persons annually to the population of the country in the early nineties and if the trend is not halted, it would not be possible to render social and economic justice to the millions of the masses. It envisaged reorientation of the health programe and its structural framework for the delivery. It was emphasized that the underprivileged themselves become the subjects of the process and merely its objects. Community based systems for a population group of 30,000 was suggested to be planned through the strengthening of the infrastructure facilities.

The National Development Council appointed a Committee on population with Shri Karunakaran as Chairman in 1991 which proposed the formulation of a National Population Policy in 1993 to take a long term holistic view of development, population growth and environmental protection and to suggest policies and guidelines for formulation of programs and a monitoring mechanism with short, medium and long term perspective and goals. An expert group on National Population Policy headed by Dr. M.S. Swaminathan appointed in 1993 to prepare a draft of national population policy, It has recommended the formation of a Population and Social Development Commission.

National Population Policy:

The National Population Policy which was announced in February 2000 seeks to initiate several measures to achieve a stable population by 2045. The 'immediate objective' of the NPP 2000 is to address the needs for contraception, health care infrastructure, and health personnel, and to provide integrated service delivery for basic reproductive and child health care. The 'medium term objective' is to bring the TFR to replacement levels by 2010, through vigorous implementation of inter-sectoral operational strategies.

The 'long term objective' is to achieve a stable population by 2045, at a level consistent with the requirements of sustainable economic growth, social development, and environmental protection. The policy includes freezing the number of seats in Lok Sabha at the current level of 543 which is based on the 1971 census till 2026, The medium term objective is to bring the total fertility rates to replacement level by 2010 through vigorous implementation of inter-sectoral operational strategies, the long term objective is to achieve a stable population by 2045, at a consistent level with the requirements of sustainable growth, social development and environmental protection.

To achieve the objectives the NPP has envisaged the following 14 socio-demographic goals for 2010:

1. Address the unmet needs for basic reproductive and child health services, supplies and infrastructure.
2. Make school education upto the age of 14, free and compulsory and reduce drop outs at primary and secondary school levels to below 20 per cent for both boys and girls.
3. Reduce infant mortality rate to below 30 per 1000 live births.
4. Reduce maternal mortality rate to below 100 per 100,000 live births.
5. Achieve universal immunization of child
6. Promote delayed marriage for girls, not earlier than the age of 18 and preferably after 20 years of age.
7. Achieve 80 per cent industrial deliveries and 100 per cent deliveries by trained persons.
8. Achieve universal access to information/counseling, and services for fertility regulation and contraception with a wide basket of choices.
9. Achieve 100 per cent registration of births, deaths, marriage and pregnancy.
10. Contain the spread of Acquired Immunodeficiency Syndrome (AIDS), and promote greater integration between the management of reproductive tract infections and sexually transmitted infections and the National AIDS Control Organization.
11. Prevent and control communicable diseases.
12. Integrate Indian Systems of Medicine (ISM) in the provision of reproductive and child health services, and in reaching out to households.
13. Promote vigorously the small family norm to achieve replacement levels of TFR.
14. Bring about convergence in implementation of related social sector programs so that family welfare becomes a people centered Programme.

In order to strengthen the Programmes of National Population Policy and to achieve the above mentioned national socio economic goals for 2020, 12 strategic themes are identified as follows:

1. Decentralized planning and programme implementation,

2. Convergence of service delivery at Village level,

3. Empowering women for improved Health and Nutrition,

4. Child health and survival,

5. Meeting the unmet needs for & family welfare and services

6. Reaching out to the underserved population groups such as urban slum dwellers, tribal communities hill areas population, displaced and migrant population; adolescents.

7. Making use of diverse health care providers.

8. Collaboration with private sector and NGOs.

9. Main streaming of Indian systems of medicine and Homeopathy.

10. Promotion of research on contraceptive technology and reproductive and child health,

11. Providing for older persons above 60 years and 12. Information's education and communications.

The population of India in 2001 has almost tripled since 1941. The growth rate of population peaked at 2.24 percent per annum in the decade of the seventies and has been gradually declining thereafter, though in absolute numbers population continues to grow at an alarming rate. The rate of growth has been less than 2 percent per annum in the period 1991- 2001.

Reasons for a high Population growth:

a. The large family size many children in a family
b. Lack of awareness among people about the hazards of a large population
c. High fertility rate and hot climate which helps increase in fertility
d. Early age of marriage, especially of girls.
e. Low death rate and high birth rate.
f. Lack of proper awareness of contraception and other family Planning measures

Family Welfare Program in India:

India, the most populous country in the world, has no more than 2.5% of global land but is the home of $1/6^{th}$ of the world's population. The prevailing high maternal, infant, childhood morbidity and mortality, low life expectancy and high fertility and associated high morbidity had been a source of concern for public health professional's right from the pre-independence period.

The Bhore Committee Report of 1946, pivotal in shaping India's health service planning, prioritized maternal and child health services, aiming to enhance their nutritional and health conditions. Notably, this report advocated for integrated primary health care services encompassing prevention, promotion, and treatment, predating the Alma Ata declaration by more than thirty years.

Under the Constitution of India elimination of poverty, ignorance and ill health are three important goals. In 1951, the infant republic took stock of the existing situation in the country and initiated the first Five Year Development Plan. Living in a resource poor country with high population density, the Planners recognized the census figures of 1951, the potential threat posed by population explosion and the need to take steps to avert it.

It was recognized that population stabilization is an essential prerequisite for sustainability of development process so that the benefits of economic development result in enhancement of the wellbeing of the people and improvement in quality of life. India became the first country in the world to formulate a National Family Planning Programme in 1952, with the objective of "reducing birth rate to the extent necessary to stabilize the population at a level consistent with requirement of national economy".

Thus, the key elements of health care to women and children and provision of contraceptive services have been the focus of India's health services right from the time of India's independence. Successive Five Year Plans have been providing the policy framework and funding for planned development of nationwide health care infrastructure and manpower. The Centrally Sponsored and 100% centrally funded Family Welfare Programme provides additional infrastructure, manpower and drugs, vaccines contraceptives and other consumables needed for improving health status of women and children and to meet all the felt needs for fertility regulation.

FAILURE OF POPULATION CONTROL POLICIES:

India is first among the countries which adopted an official family planning programme, as early as 1950. However, fifty years later it could not prevent the population touching the one billion mark. It is obvious that despite good intentions and concerted efforts we have failed in controlling our population. Considering the seriousness of the situation, it is appropriate to introspect and ascertain as to what went wrong. The problem, though very complex, can be discussed under two headings: (i) the available methods for contraception and (ii) the users.

It is obvious now that there cannot be an ideal contraceptive, suitable for everybody. A careful choice has to be made among the current available methods, depending on the gender, country, socio- religious and cultural practices. According to available information the most accepted methods are the two terminal methods, vasectomy in the case of the male, and tubectomy in the case of the female. These are methods of choice for all those who have completed their family size and to use them is a conscious decision made by the couple.

The next most commonly used methods are the barrier methods, still popular in spite of a high failure rate. The other methods such as the use of contraceptive pills, intrauterine devices and injectable are used by a relatively small percentage of the population. It is also evident that except for the barrier method and vasectomy there are no methods available for male contraception, in contrast to the variety of methods available and in use for the female. Does this mean that the available methods are not adequate for the requirements and this inadequacy is the reason for uncontrolled population growth? The answer is firmly in the negative.

The available methods are more than adequate but what is lacking is the will to use them. This brings in the philosophical question as to what is meant by will and why the will is not there. It is for this reason that it was mentioned earlier that the issue of the user is a complex one. The users are both male and female, and with limited options available to the male, the entire burden of limiting the family is shouldered by the female. However, except for a miniscule percentage of the female population, the majority are passive participants in the process with no decision-making capacity. It is in this context that population control was given a new dimension, namely reproductive health, which to a large extent centers on the female. The concept of reproductive health recognizes the diversity of the special health needs of women before, during, and beyond child bearing age, as well as the needs of men and the quality of life of the people involved.

If the population continues to increase at its current rate, it will inevitably devastate the country. The government's lack of initiative, coupled with the indifference of the Indian population, bears responsibility for this impending crisis. Many are oblivious to the severity of the situation. Eventually, this neglect will lead to riots and conflicts over scarce resources like food and water. India risks becoming the world's largest generator of slums, with cities resembling chaotic marketplaces teeming with people. Traffic will resemble an ant colony in

motion, amid a cacophony of screams and shouts that no one heeds.

THE CHALLENGES AHEAD:

India's per capita income has doubled over the past 20 years. With population growth slowing now to about 1.6 per cent per annum, a growth rate of the gross domestic product (GDP) of around 9 per cent per annum would be sufficient to quadruple the per capita income by 2020. Opinions on achievable rates of economic growth have a tendency to swing along with the short-term economic performances. Few years ago, the global boom, the IT revolution and the all-round optimism led many to believe that in the coming decade, India could mimic the 9-10 per cent growth rates that China achieved over a twenty year period. Such optimism is out of fashion today.

But there is ample evidence showing that if we can adopt a longer term perspective that is not blinded by immediate circumstances and fluctuating moods, higher rates of growth should be achievable for India in the coming years. This is not a prediction—it is a potential. The reality will depend on how effectively we seize the opportunity to do so. From a historical perspective, global rates of development have been increasing for more than a century. The dramatic rise of Japan and the East Asian tigers, and most recently China, are illustrative of this point. An objective assessment reveals that all the major engines of economic growth that have accelerated growth up till now, will be present in greater abundance in the coming years than they had been in the past.

SUMMARY:

Rapid population growth continues to be a matter of concern for the country as it has manifold effects, one of the most important being environment degradation. The outcomes of excessive population are industrialization and urbanization. The study reveals that rapid population growth has led to the over-exploitation of natural resources. The deforestation has led to the shrinking of forest cover, which eventually affects human health. The considerable magnitude of air pollution in the country also pulls up the number of people suffering from respiratory diseases and many a times leading to deaths and serious health hazards. The situation is also similar for water pollution, as both ground water and surface water contamination leads to various water borne diseases. From the various effects of environmental degradation on human beings, discussed in this paper, it appears that if human beings wants to exist on earth, there is now high time to give top priority to control pollution of all types for a healthy living. It can be said that even after fifty years of independence, India is unable to achieve the desirable standards of health for its population as consequences of environment degradation. What is desired is the will of the people as well as the cooperation of the Government to promote family planning methods.

GLOSSARY:

1. **Population:** A population is the number of living things that live together in the same place. A city's population is the number of people living in that city. These people are called inhabitants or residents.
2. **Policy:** A policy is a deliberate system of principles to guide decisions and achieve rational outcomes. A policy is a statement of intent, and is implemented as a procedure or protocol. Policies are generally adopted by a governance body within an organization.
3. **Over Population:** Overpopulation occurs when a species' population exceeds the carrying capacity of its ecological niche. It can result from an increase in births (fertility rate), a decline in the mortality rate, an increase in immigration, or an unsustainable biome and depletion of resources.
4. **Optimum Population:** Optimum population has been defined as that size of population enabling per capita output of the maximum orders accompanied by the highest possible standards of living under a given set of economic and technological conditions.
5. **Under Population:** Under population exists when a population is too small, therefore unable to fully utilize the available resource endowments. Under population is also characterized by a situation where the available resources are capable of supporting a much larger population with no reduction in living standards. The situation is found in regions of low technical development such as equatorial Congo, Amazon River basin or the rich Prairie region of North America.
6. **Family Welfare System:** Child and Family Welfare System comprise of laws and policies, programmes, services, practices and structures designed to promote the well-being of children by ensuring safety and protection from harm; achieving permanency and strengthening families to care for their children.

CHECK YOUR PROGRESS:

1. The main solution to solve the population problem in India is to control the birth rate.
2. According to the transition theory of population, population remains stable by increasing or decreasing the birth rate in the initial stage.
3. India's rapidly increasing population has become the most serious problem in its economic development.
4. Family planning was first adopted in India in 1961-66.
5. The Chairman of the Health Survey and Development Committee was Mr. Joseph Bhore.
6. India's population growth was recognized in the first five year plan itself.
7. In 1953 the number of family planning clinics was 165.
8. The objective of the Third Five Year Plan was to stabilize population growth.
9. In the fourth five-year plan, the birth rate was to be reduced to 32 persons per 1000.
10. Internal emergency was declared in the country in June 1976.

REFERENCES:

1. Dhingra, I.C., Garg, V.K., Economic Development and Planning in India, (15[th]edn.), 2002, Sultan Chand & Sons, New Delhi
2. Misra, S.K., Puri, V.K., Indian Economy, (25[th]edn.), 2007, Himalaya PublishingHouse, Mumbai
3. Chandna, R.C. (2000) A Population Geography. Kalyani Press: New Delhi
4. Clarke, J.I. (1972). Population Geography. Oxford: Pergamon Press
5. Peters, G.L. and R.P. Larkin (1979). Population Geography: Problem, Concepts and Prospects. Dubuque, Lowa
6. Hussain, M (2009). Human Geography. Rawat Publication: New Delhi
7. Tiwari, R.C. (2011). Geography of India. Prayag Pustak Bhawan: Allahabad
8. http://indiabudget.nic.in/es2001-02/chapt2002/tab91.pdf

9. http://www.popline.org/docs/1490/190029.html
10. http://www.usaid.gov/in/programareas/environm.html
11. http://indiabudget.nic.in/es2001-02/chapt2002/tab91.pdf
12. http://www.india2020.org.in/category/india2020/report/
13. http://planningcommission.nic.in/reports/wrkpapers/
    wp_hwpaper.pdf

TERMINAL QUESTION:

A. Long Questions

1. Describe population problem in India
2. What do you understand by optimum population, elaborate with suitable examples and diagram?
3. Evaluate population policy in India
4. Explain role of Five Years Plan in Population Management in India.
5. Give your views on population Management and policy improvement for India

B. Short Questions

1. What are the major causes of the population problems in India?
2. How does India's rapidly growing population affect the country's economy and resources?
3. What government policies and initiatives have been implemented to address the population problem in India?
4. What are the potential long-term consequences if the population problem in India is not effectively managed?
5. What are the key population policies and initiatives that the Indian government has implemented to control population growth?
6. How effective have family planning programs, such as the National Family Planning Program, been in India's population policies?
7. What role does education and awareness play in India's population policies, particularly in addressing issues like gender inequality and family planning?

8. How do population policies in India balance the need for controlling population growth with ensuring the well-being and rights of its citizens?

C. **Multiple Choice Questions**

1. What is the primary reason for India's high population growth rate?

a. Increased birth rates
b. Decreased immigration
c. Increased death rates
d. Improved healthcare

(Answers: a)

2. Which state in India has the highest population density?

a. Uttar Pradesh
b. Maharashtra
c. Bihar
d. Kerala

(Answers: a)

3. The National Population Policy of India emphasizes:

a. Encouraging a higher birth rate
b. Promoting smaller families
c. Restricting healthcare access
d. Limiting educational opportunities

(Answers: b)

4. What is the legal age for marriage in India for males and females, respectively?

a. 18 and 21
b. 18 and 18

c. 21 and 21

d. 21 and 18

(Answers: a)

5. Which of the following factors contributes to India's gender imbalance due to son preference?

a. Equal opportunities for girls and boys

b. Gender-neutral family planning policies

c. Traditional dowry practices

d. Strict laws against gender discrimination

(Answers: c)

6. Which organization is primarily responsible for implementing population policies in India?

a. WHO (World Health Organization)

b. UNICEF (United Nations International Children's Emergency Fund)

c. NITI Aayog

d. Ministry of Finance

Answers: c

7. In which year was the "Jansankhya Sthirata Kosh" (National Population Stabilization Fund) established in India?

a. 1947

b. 1981

c. 2000

d. 2010

(Answers: c)

8. What is the goal of India's National Health Mission in relation to population policies?

a. Reducing the availability of healthcare services
b. Increasing maternal and child mortality
c. Providing accessible and quality healthcare, including family planning
d. Promoting traditional medicine over modern healthcare

(Answers: c)

CHAPTER FIVE

AGRICULTURAL INFRASTRUCTURE DEVELOPMENT

INTRODUCTION:

India, primarily an agrarian nation, relies heavily on agriculture as the cornerstone of its economy and livelihoods. Despite a significant decline in its contribution to the Gross National Product, agriculture remains fundamental to India's economic framework and continues to support a substantial portion of the population through employment. In 1950-51, approximately 69.5% of India's workforce was engaged in agriculture and allied activities. By the 2015-16 economic review, this figure had decreased to 48.9%, yet more than half of India's population still depends directly on these sectors for their livelihoods.

Agriculture forms the basis for various industries such as cotton textiles, sugarcane, edible oils, and food processing, providing crucial raw materials. It remains a vital source of income and employment, supporting agricultural-based industries across the country. India's cultural fabric, spanning from east to west and north to south, is deeply intertwined with agricultural cycles, reflected in numerous festivals.

Despite its reduced percentage in the GDP and overall employment, agriculture plays a significant role in India's total exports, contributing valuable foreign exchange. It is intricately linked to food security and nutritional needs, essential for the well-being of the masses. Achieving social security and economic development goals hinges on sustaining healthy agricultural production through various critical factors.

THE AGRICULTURAL INFRASTRUCTURE DEVELOPMENT:

THE AGRICULTURE:

India is a country of the great climatic diversity; situated in tropical and temperate zones. These favorable conditions make available more than 55% of its land for agriculture. Most of the countries of the world raise only one crop in the year but India has the privilege to produce two or more crops in different parts of the country. So that huge diversity in crops too are inevitable, one side tropical crops like rice, sugarcane, peanut, banana are easily cultivated in the country and on other side temperate crops like cotton, wheat, soybean, are produced efficiently. Indian agriculture dominated by the production of food crops (64.18% of cropped land) and phenomenal area (about 30% of cropped land) is available for fodder crops, pastures, cash crops and other allied activities. Due to the huge diversity of physical and climatic conditions different crops are grown here in the country can be grouped as:

Food Crops:

India is the country of more than 140 crores of population (as approximated by the Indian Govt), thus there is a continuous demand for food crops throughout the country. People generally prefer to grow crops that are in continuous demand and available market. Indian agriculture is mainly of subsistence type and main motive of population is to fulfill the food demands of the family. Thus major part of the agricultural land in India is covered by the food crops. Rice, wheat, maize, pulses like gram, and tur, jowar and bajra are the important crops produced in India. These crops are grown all over the country and throughout the year. Three crops of rice are raised in the states of Assam and West Bengal. Fields remain hardly vacant where there is irrigation facilities are available.

Cash Crops/Commercial Crops:

These are the crops raised for sale in a raw and semi-processed form to generate income by the farmers. These crops include sugarcane, groundnut, soybean, mustard, etc. They provide raw materials to a large number of agro-based industries in India and fetch more income to the farmers as compared to other crops.

Drinkable Items:

Tea, coffee, and tobacco are the main drinkable items produced in different regions of India; mostly in Assam, Kerala, and many others. These are also important cash crops.

Fibers:

Cotton, jute and mesta, etc. are the fibers used as raw material in different agro-based industries are the important commercial crops grown mainly in West Bengal, Gujarat, and Maharashtra states.

Determinants of Agriculture in India:

Agriculture in India is determined by various factors comprising physical, institutional and technological factors etc. Physical factors which determine agriculture in India are topography, climate, soils etc. Institutional factors are size of farms, land tenure system, and technical factors include irrigational facilities, use of High Yield Variety (HYV) seeds, fertilizers, farm machinery, pesticides/insecticides etc. All these have collective impacts on the development of agriculture, crop production land productivity in the country.

MAIN FEATURES OF INDIAN AGRICULTURE:

India is predominantly an agricultural country but conditions of farmers and agriculture both are poor. As compared to world average of only 11 % land available for agriculture, India is in very advantageous conditions as about 55% India's land is available for farming. But due to poor productivity, dominance of food crops, intensive subsistence type of agriculture and poor institutional and technological developments, Indian farmers are not sound much economically. Agriculture in India is not economically viable presently leaving some exceptions of big farmers. Continuous higher rates of population growth are making this situation more complicated. In spite of huge technological advancements in agricultural machinery and technology all over the world, Indian farmers are still dependent on traditional agricultural methods, tools and techniques.

Modernization of farming in India is still limited to big and economically sound farmers. In India, agriculture is still of subsistence type and agricultural productivity is very low as compared to the developed countries of the world. Main objectives of Indian farmers' are still to fulfill their family needs; only surplus production is available for marketing. Commercialization of agriculture in India is very limited and restricted to a very few crops. Poor Indian farmers are not in conditions to use much oriented technology, HYV seeds, and chemical fertilizers. Small size of land holdings and faulty tenure system are proving hazardous to the agriculture in India. Main characteristics of Indian agriculture can be grouped as follows:

1. Ever-increasing pressure of population.
2. Poor productivity of crops.
3. Dependent on monsoon.
4. Unbalanced distribution of land among farmers.
5. Ill defined tenure system.
6. Intensive agriculture.
7. Small size of land holdings.
8. Highly diversified agriculture.
9. Dominance of food crops.
10. Traditional methods of farming.
11. Problematic nature of Indian agriculture.
12. Poor technological advancements as compared to developed countries.
13. Poor crop commercialization.
14. Illiterate and unaware farmers.
15. Poor risk bearing capacity of the farmers.

THE INFRASTRUCTURE DEVELOPMENT

Agriculture is affect by many factors like, natural, institutional and infrastructural, etc. Topography, relief, climate, and soils are the major natural factors decide the agriculture of any area, country or region. Whereas irrigation, seeds, fertilizers, energy and power sources like petrol, diesel, electricity etc. are the major infrastructural factors play an important role in agriculture and crop production. For the growth, development, and healthy agricultural practices and also for desired crop production, agricultural infrastructure is must. Without the availability of desired and up to the mark infrastructure, production of crops suffers a lot. Thus it is important to have a look of the agriculture related infrastructure and their status in India.

Role of Agricultural Infrastructure in Regional Development:

Region is a differentiated segment of the earth surface having some similarities and can be differentiated from other nearby area easily on the basis of some specific characteristics. Regional development refers to develop an economically and socially backward area with special aids and assistance. Rural infrastructure provide base for extensively improving the quality of life in the rural areas by accelerating the process of agricultural development. Agricultural infrastructure projects, in general, need high financial support, with high risk whereas low rate of returns on investments. Agricultural infrastructure has direct connections with the farmers' access to institutional finance and markets, and increasing crop yields, for instance adequate money helps in promoting agricultural production quantitatively as well as qualitatively. Agricultural infrastructure keeps the potential to renovate and modernize the traditional agriculture practices or subsistence agriculture into modern, profitable and dynamic farming system in India.

Agricultural infrastructure is considered to have wide range of services and aids that facilitate the agricultural production, procurement, and processing of agricultural products, and also conservation and trade of such products. Agricultural infrastructure may be grouped under following categories -

Input based infrastructure: Seeds, fertilizers, pesticides, farm equipments and machinery etc.

Resource based infrastructure: Irrigation facilities and energy sources

Physical infrastructure: Road network, transportation, storage, processing, preservation, etc.

Institutional infrastructure: Financial services and banking, marketing, information, advertisement and communication services, research and development in agriculture (R&D), extension services, awareness and education of farmers etc.

Agriculturists and economists have recognized the growing importance of agricultural infrastructure in overall development of the agriculture in India. They are sure that its role not only limited to agricultural development but also broadened up-to the livelihood, food and nutritional security of the population and future economic developments of the country. In this regard eleven components of infrastructure have been identified which are - irrigational facilities, peoples' access to drinking water, good means of transportation, credit and financial institutions, efficient storage services for crops, trade and commercial infrastructure, processing units, public services, agricultural research and extension services, communication and information services, land conservation services, health and education services. These are the basic amenities must be available for village development and ultimately the agricultural developments.

India is the country of severe heterogeneity where diversity and disparity in economy, polity, society and culture are at climax. After independence feelings were on high for economic, cultural and social development of the Indian population. During the initial phases of planning, the main emphasis was on overall national development so the approaches and ideas of time bound planning were adopted, formulated and implemented. But after short while, keeping in mind the high diversity of soils, vegetation, relief and socio-economic conditions in the country; concept of regional development gained the momentum which ensures better utilization of highly differential geographical and agro-climatic potentialities across the various regions in India.

Each region demands different plan and policy, different agricultural equipment and infrastructure, tools and technology. Efficient regional development heavily resides on availability, accessibility and status of agricultural infrastructure. Regions having efficient agricultural infrastructure are agriculturally developed and economically sound and regions lacking these facilities are lagging behind in the country for instance Punjab, Haryana and western Uttar Pradesh is developed only due to their developed agricultural infrastructure.

Investments like irrigation, fertilizers, energy and seeds are the backbone of the agriculture in India. Future of Indian agriculture, its sustainability and food security of Indian population very much depend on them.

IRRIGATION:

Among many other infrastructural factors, irrigation is an important factor for agriculture in India. In fact, irrigation is the base of modern agriculture. Supply of water to the crops, artificially, in absence of rainfall is known as 'irrigation'. Without adequate irrigation agricultural production suffers much and quality of crops also sacrifices. In Indian scenario where agriculture is very much depends on monsoonal rain, which is very irregular and uncertain and of limited nature; irrigation is more important for proper production of crops. Besides this rainfall in India is unevenly distributed i.e. different regions, states and areas in India receive different amount of rainfall.

All these factors increase the role of irrigation in India. Various crops need different amount of water and crops like rice, sugarcane, Jute and various horticultural crops need much amount of water regularly. Due to the huge importance and need of water Government of India has established Water Irrigation Department, Water Resource Ministry and National Water Policy was decided to facilitate, manage and fix appropriate use of available water resources in the country. Irrigation in India includes a network of major and minor canals from perennial and seasonal rivers, use of groundwater: well and tube well based systems, ponds/tanks, and rainwater harvesting projects for agricultural activities.

Among them groundwater based irrigation system is the largest. It is estimated that in 2013-14, only about 47.7% of total agricultural land in India was reliably irrigated. About $2/3^{rd}$ cultivated land in India is dependent on monsoons. Irrigation in India has helped in sufficient crop production, improved agricultural productivity, and improved food security, less dependence on monsoons, and also created several agriculture based job opportunities. Dams; constructed to support irrigation, produce electricity and water based transport facilities, and also provide drinking water to the growing population, and help in controlling floods and frequent droughts in the country.

Need of Irrigation in India:

Need of irrigation specifically in India rises due to the various factors which are as follows:

1. Uncertainty of rainfall
2. Long monsoonal gap
3. Irregularity of rainfall
4. Limited duration of rainfall
5. Uncertainty of monsoon burst and retreat
6. Torrential nature of rainfall
7. Some specific crops need higher amount of water
8. Commercial crops need more water
9. HYV's need regular irrigation
10. Different nature of soil throughout the country
11. Presence of dry areas and regions in the country

Facilities of Irrigation in India:

Indian climate is tropical monsoonal and country receive most of its rainfall due to monsoonal rainfall. Irrigation is must for proper agricultural practices throughout the country. Geographical and geological conditions are favorable in India for constructing various means of irrigation leaving some parts in the country as;

1. Perennial Rivers
2. Soft sedimentary soils
3. Fertile land
4. Abundance of Plains
5. High underground water table
6. Abundance and suitability of ponds in South India.
7. Continuous need for irrigation due to large number of agro-climatic zones

The above mentioned factors have supported the development of a large irrigation networks in the country, whether it may be canals, wells, tube wells, ponds/tanks or small or giant dams. All collectively and individually support the irrigation and ensure proper crop production.

Means of irrigation in India:

Due to the geological, topographical, and climatic variations, different means of irrigation are in practice in India, which are as follows:

Canals:

Canals are the major source of irrigation in India and about 25% of total irrigated land in India is covered by canal irrigation. It is cheaper as compared to the other irrigation sources. Plain surface is suitable for canal formation. Canals are spread throughout the country but major concentration of canals is seen mostly in the states of Uttar Pradesh, Punjab, and Bihar. Canals are mainly of two types; perennial and seasonal canals. The longest canal in India is Indira Gandhi Canal, which is about 650 km long. The maximum part of the total irrigated area of the country by canals is in Uttar Pradesh followed by Punjab and Haryana. About 165.97 lakh hectare land of India was irrigated by canals during the year 2008-09 from which half of the irrigated land concentrated in the Northern plains of India. Other major states where irrigation is done by the canals are Haryana, Punjab, Madhya Pradesh, Bihar, and Andhra Pradesh. Canal provides irrigation to 91.72 % of irrigated area in Jammu & Kashmir, 64.7 % in Orissa, 66.24 % in Chhattisgarh, 44.28% in Haryana and 34.63 % irrigated area of Andhra Pradesh is irrigated by canals.

Major canals of India which are providing irrigation to a large part of the country are as follows:

- **Sutlej-Yamuna link Canal:** Sutlej Yamuna link canal is about 214 km long freight canal which links Sutlej and Yamuna rivers and canal also known as SYL.

- **Sirhind Canal:** It irrigates the areas of Punjab and Haryana.
- **Indira Gandhi Canal:** It irrigates the districts of Ganganagar, Bikaner, Jodhpur and Jaisalmer in Rajasthan.
- **Buckingham Canal:** It irrigates Andhra Pradesh and Tamil Nadu
- **Triveni Canal:** It irrigates the agricultural lands in Bihar
- **Upper Ganga Canal:** Uttarakhand and Uttar Pradesh
- **Lower Ganga Canal:** Uttarakhand and Uttar Pradesh
- **Kaveri-Vaigai link Canal:** Kerala, Karnataka and Tamil Nadu
- **Agra Canal:** Uttar Pradesh, Haryana and Rajasthan
- **Sarda Canal:** It irrigates the land in Uttar Pradesh.
- **Eden Canal:** It has been taken out from the river Damodar in West Bengal.
- **Tilpara Dam Canal:** It irrigates the areas of West Bengal.
- **Mutha Canal:** It has been taken out from the river Mutha near Khadagwasala (Pune) in Maharashtra.
- **Sampad Sagar Canal:** It irrigates the areas of Andhra Pradesh.

Wells:

Wells for irrigation are in use from ancient time throughout India but major concentration of wells can be easily noticed in northern India mainly from Punjab to Bihar. Besides this wells are also used in eastern Rajasthan, Gujarat, Andhra Pradesh, Karnataka, Maharashtra, Tamil Nadu, and Madhya Pradesh. Wells are the cheap means of irrigation for poor Indian farmers. In 1950-51 about 50 lakh wells were in the country and presently their numbers goes more than 150 lakhs.

Tube wells:

The use of tube wells in India began only after 1930, primarily in regions where canal construction was impractical. However, more recently, tube wells have become prevalent across most Indian states, especially in areas rich in underground water resources. Wells and tube wells combined now support 58% of the country's irrigated land.

While wells and tube wells offer numerous advantages, such as ready availability of water, their drawbacks are significant. These include limited coverage area for irrigation, susceptibility to drying up, high initial investment in terms of both money and labor, declining groundwater levels, and their ineffectiveness in regions with saline groundwater.

Despite their widespread adoption and benefits, the challenges associated with well and tube well irrigation underscore thc need for sustainable water management practices in India.

Ponds:

Ponds are depressions on the earth's surface where rainwater collects, and they can be either natural or man-made. Southern India, particularly states like Tamil Nadu, Karnataka, Orissa, Jharkhand, Uttar Pradesh, and Rajasthan, plays a significant role in pond irrigation, with a substantial amount of land being irrigated through ponds. Ponds contribute to about 3.4% of total irrigation in India.

The positive aspects of pond irrigation include the fact that many ponds in India are natural, requiring no investment for construction. Even artificial ponds are relatively inexpensive to dig. Ponds also support fisheries, providing an additional source of income and nutrition.

However, there are challenges associated with pond irrigation. Ponds tend to dry up during hot summers, reducing their reliability as a water source. They also accumulate sediment due to annual rainfall, which requires periodic dredging to maintain their capacity. Additionally, ponds typically provide limited irrigation coverage compared to other methods. So, while pond irrigation offers several advantages such as low cost and potential for fisheries, it also presents challenges like seasonal drying and sedimentation that need to be managed for sustainable use of water resources in India.

Dams:

Dams are the larger from of ponds; constructed manually and rain or river water stored in them which is used for irrigation, drinking and also for electricity generation. Bhakara Nangal, Heerakund, Tehri, and Rihand are the important dams of India.

POWER:

Power resources are the base of industrial as well as agricultural development of any country. With the modernization of agriculture and increasing use of modern energy driven tools in agriculture, importance of power sources in agriculture is increasing day by day. In modern age of industrialization and mechanization, status and scope of power resources are the indicators of economic development of any country. Countries are considered powerful and developed because of their power resources and their developmental status. There are mainly two type of power resources are available are as under:

- **Renewable Energy resources:** are those which can be used again and again. For example water energy, wind energy, tidal energy and vegetation, etc. are the renewable energy sources. Most of them are non conventional sources of energy in India.
- **Non-renewable energy resources:** are those which can be used only once i.e. they exhaust after single use. Coal, petroleum, and natural gas are the non-renewable energy sources. These all are conventional sources of energy and their use is very common.

With the development of irrigational facilities, use of HYV's seeds, and frequent use of fertilizers; mechanization of agricultural activities is at large scale in India. Animal and human labor replaced by the tractors, threshers, harvesters, energy driven tube wells, etc. All these need a large amount of power for operation. Power sources are frequently in use in running machinery in agriculture. Machines like tractors and pumping sets run by petroleum, while tube wells, run by electricity. Diesel is more costly product for poor farmers as compared to electricity. Cheap and regular electricity is important in decreasing input cost by the farmers. There are huge crises of electricity supply. Demand is higher and production and supply are lower. In the year 1950-51 only 3.9% electricity was used for agricultural activities, which increased to 21.7% in 2006-07. There is huge demand of electricity in agricultural activities; and agricultural growth may suffer negatively in the absence of proper supply of electricity in agriculture sector. Rural Electrification Corporation was established in 1969 to facilitate electricity in the rural areas of the country. Subsidies are common in rural villages. States like Haryana and Punjab are using more than 40% of their electricity for agricultural purposes and the use of electricity is increasing continuously in the other Indian states such as Uttar Pradesh, Bihar, Gujarat, Karnataka, Tamil Nadu, and Rajasthan etc.

FERTILIZERS:

With the irrigation and improved seeds, fertilizers also beneficial in producing crops in ample amount and is an important investment in agriculture. Appropriate uses of fertilizers facilitate positive growth in crop production. Nitrogen, Phosphorus, and Potash are the main three fertilizers used in agriculture, besides various micro-nutrients. Tremendous growth has been seen in the production, import and use of fertilizers after Green Revolution in India. Country is just after USA and China in use and production of fertilizers in the world. The use of fertilizers in India was very limited before Green Revolution but after it, the use of chemical fertilizers increased in leaps and bonds. It the increased to 24909 thousand ton in 2008-09 from only 16788 thousand ton in the year 1960-61.

Per hectare use of fertilizers has increased many folds after Green Revolution but it is very less as compared to other developed countries of the world. In the year 2008-09 per hectare use of fertilizers were 129.2 kg. There are ample scope for increasing fertilizers use and also crop production in India. Huge variations are obvious in the use of fertilizers in India, states like Punjab, Haryana, Uttar Pradesh, Andhra Pradesh and Tamil Nadu are using fertilizers in huge amount per hectare whereas states as Arunachal Pradesh, Sikkim, Uttarakhand, Mizoram and Nagaland are using very low amount of chemical fertilizers per hectare. Use of fertilizers like Nitrogen, Phosphorus and Potash should do in the ratio of 4:2:1 for most crops but huge variation is seen in use due to lack of awareness of the farmers resulting in poor crop production and various soil related problems.

SEEDS

Seeds are the major part in agriculture throughout the world as seeds decide the ultimate quality and quantity of agricultural production. In this sense role of High Yielding variety (HYV) seeds are more important and essential asset and investment in agriculture. Use of improved varieties of seeds in different agro-climatic regions of India can support increased production.

First a HYV seeds of wheat was developed in Mexico and further Indian scientists developed improved varieties of wheat from Mexican wheat Lerma Rajo, Sonora-63 and 64 and Kalayan Sona are suitable in Indian agro-climatic conditions. These improved seeds were the torch bearer of Green Revolution in India. Improved variety of rice IR-8 developed by the International Rice Research Institute, Philippines in the decade of 1960. IR-8 rice seeds were found suitable for geographical conditions of India. After that HYV seeds of sugarcane, pulses, cotton, and various other crops were developed and successfully diffused in India.

For this purpose, Indian seed development programmes were adopted and various institutes were established at the state and national level to support the development. Contributions of Indian Council of Agricultural Research (ICAR), various private, government and co- operatives are valuable. Universities like Chandra Shekhar Azad Agricultural University, Kanpur, G.B. Pant Agriculture University, Pant Nagar, Faizabad Agriculture University, and many more are continuously working towards modified seed production.

National Seeds Corporation (NSC) established in 1963 (19th March), State Farms Corporation (SFC), State Seed Corporation (SSC) and more than 100 privately owned companies are continuously working in the field of seed improvement, up-gradation and modifications. Besides these, various state seed certification agencies, research laboratories are also working for seed certification and related research. In the years 2008-09 about 19000 thousand quintal certified seeds were distributed to the farmers, the amount of certified seeds distributed were only 5750 thousand quintal in the year 1991-92, thus amount of certified seeds are increasing continuously.

Characteristics of Improved/Hybrid Seeds:

1. Suitable for the use of fertilizers.
2. Short maturation period of crops.
3. Adequate utilization of irrigation.
4. Employment Generation.
5. Ease of use.
6. Better yield.
7. Greater uniformity.
8. Improved color and quality.
9. Disease resistance.
10. Higher income.

But various problems are also linked with the improved varieties of seeds. Lower water table, higher use of fertilizers and pesticides, required better infrastructure, financial crises, poor mechanization, and lacked extension services; markets and storage, health issues, poor by- products and various environmental problems are linked with HYV's of seeds in India. Main deficiencies of HYV's seeds programme are as:

1. Seeds not tested and certified scientifically due to lack of developed seed testing mechanism in India. So that a huge amount of uncertified seeds are being sell in the market every year causing poor production.
2. Ignorance of crops like pulses and oilseeds as main emphasis of these programmes is on wheat and rice seeds.
3. Genetically modified seeds are not environmentally viable and their various health impacts are not tested yet.

4. Autonomy of big companies is prevalent and these seeds are much costly and inaccessible to poor and marginal Indian farmers.
5. Diversity of crops is also at risk.
6. Risk of Bio-piracy.

Problems linked with Indian agriculture:

The agricultural landscape in India has witnessed significant developments since independence, spanning across various dimensions. There has been a substantial expansion of agricultural land, marked increases in crop production and productivity, and numerous institutional and technical advancements. Despite these strides, however, Indian farmers continue to face profound challenges, leading to persistently low living standards that fall short of dignified levels.

Several critical issues underscore the current state of Indian agriculture. The rural population is increasingly abandoning agriculture as a livelihood, exacerbated by inadequate land reforms and prevailing problems of landlordism and tenancy. Many agricultural workers do not own the land they cultivate, contributing to fragmented land holdings that shrink further over time. Poor infrastructure, including insufficient irrigation and transportation facilities, remains a significant impediment to agricultural progress. Moreover, government support and investment in agriculture are often inadequate, with low rates of crop commercialization and a persistent reliance on subsistence farming methods.

Traditional and sometimes out-dated agricultural practices persist alongside insufficient focus on allied sectors such as livestock and fisheries. Storage and processing facilities for agricultural products are inadequate, leading to substantial post-harvest losses. Government capital investment in agriculture remains low, exacerbating the economic challenges faced by small and uneconomic farmers. Despite efforts, crop diversification remains limited, and agricultural productivity struggles with heavy dependence on monsoon rains, highlighting vulnerability to climate variability.

In summation, while there have been notable advances, agriculture in India today is more often a necessity than a pursuit driven by passion. Addressing these multifaceted challenges requires comprehensive reforms and sustained investment across the agricultural value chain to ensure sustainable livelihoods and food security for India's rural population.

Steps to check the agricultural problems:

India is a developing country and agriculture is still mainstay of employment of population in India. Various problems are linked with the Indian agriculture discussed above. To minimize and solve these problems, prevalent in Indian agriculture, following steps should be taken:

1. Facilitation of adequate and efficient irrigational facilities.
2. Provision of cheap and proper electricity supply and petroleum availability.
3. Cheap and accessible HYV seeds to the poor farmers.
4. Proper and desired supply of fertilizers.
5. Development of transportation network, storage facilities.
6. Proper trade and commerce facilities.
7. Consolidation of landholdings.
8. Adequate and easy capital.
9. Crop commercialization.
10. Viable price fixation of produce.
11. Ceiling of land.
12. Removal of intermediaries.
13. Awareness among farmers.
14. Administrative and political support.
15. Provision of subsidies. and
16. Farm mechanization etc.

Economic Survey indicates that the government is keen interested on doubling the farmers' income and launched several new initiatives that encompass activities from seed to marketing. Soil Health Card, Input Management, Per Drop More Crop in Pradhan Mantri Krishi Sinchai Yojana (PMKSY), Pradhan Mantri Fasal Bima Yojana (PMFBY), online trading platform for agricultural commodities in India (e-NAM) etc, are the good initiations of Government in this regard.

SUMMARY:

Agriculture remains the cornerstone of livelihood for a significant portion of India's population, even after more than 75 years of independence. Despite extensive diversification into other economic sectors, agriculture continues to occupy a substantial role in India's economy. In 1950-51, approximately 69.5% of India's workforce was engaged in agriculture and related activities. By the 2015-16 economic review, although this figure had decreased to 48.9% of total employment, more than half of India's population still directly depends on agriculture and allied sectors for their sustenance.

India's agricultural sector supports various industries that rely on agricultural raw materials, thereby providing a crucial base for the country's agro-based industries. Agriculture also contributes significantly to India's GDP and total exports, fetching valuable foreign exchange. Furthermore, it plays a vital role in ensuring food security and meeting the nutritional requirements of the Indian population. The country's diverse climatic zones, ranging from tropical to temperate, facilitate efficient production of a wide array of crops such as rice, sugarcane, peanuts, bananas, cotton, wheat, soybeans, and mangoes.

Despite considerable infrastructural developments including irrigation, modernization of tools and techniques, and innovations, Indian agriculture faces numerous challenges. These include small and fragmented land holdings, unclear land ownership and tenancy laws, inadequate irrigation facilities, heavy reliance on monsoon rains, outdated farm machinery, lack of farmer awareness, and diminishing interest among the younger generation in pursuing agriculture as a career.

Since independence, Indian agriculture has witnessed substantial transformations, yet the benefits have not reached a majority of small-scale farmers. Infrastructure remains underdeveloped and inaccessible in many regions, leaving farmers highly vulnerable to the unpredictability of monsoons. Irrigation systems often suffer from water shortages, particularly in canals during certain months. Additionally, insufficient and untimely power and energy supply force farmers to rely heavily on expensive diesel, exacerbating financial hardships.

High-yielding varieties (HYVs) of seeds and modern farming technologies are predominantly accessible to larger farmers, exacerbating disparities in agricultural productivity. Financial instability among farmers persists, aggravated by unbalanced use of chemical fertilizers that degrade soil fertility, and uncontrolled irrigation practices leading to siltation and waterlogging in fertile lands.

Addressing these challenges demands significant investment in agriculture, including improved credit facilities, enhanced infrastructure, and better market access to increase crop production and raise farmers' incomes. Farmer awareness and extension services play a pivotal role in promoting sustainable agricultural practices and transforming agriculture into a profitable venture across India.

GLOSSARY:

1. **GDP-** Gross Domestic Product.
2. **Cash Crops-** crops which are grown for sale to return a profit.
3. **HYV seeds-** High Yielding variety seeds.
4. **Regional development-** it is a broad term includes the provision of aid and assistance to the regions for their economic development.
5. **Input-** What is put in or taken in the process of agricultural production.
6. **Irrigation-** providing water artificially to the crops.
7. **Perennial Rivers-** stream flow all around the year.
8. **Seasonal Rivers-** stream flow for few months mainly in rainy season.
9. **Agro-Climatic Zones-** a land unit climatically suitable for a certain range of crops with its unique climate and crop growing period.
10. **Renewable-** source of energy that is not depleted by use.
11. **Non-renewable-** source of energy that is depleted by use.
12. **Mechanization-** process of moving from work by hand/animals to the work with machinery.
13. **Fertilizers-** substance added to soil to increase its fertility.
14. **Bio-piracy-** unlawful commercial exploitation of biological materials.
15. **Crop commercialization-** production of crops for sale in the market, rather than for family consumption.
16. **NAM-** National Agriculture Market.

CHECK YOUR PROGRESS:

1. India's climate is of diverse type.
2. India has the largest farmer population in the world.
3. India's agriculture is mainly of discharge type.
4. Tea Coffee Tobacco is the included main beverage crop.
5. Cash crops include sugarcane, groundnut, mustard and soybean.
6. Agricultural factors in India are determined by the climate here.
7. About 55% of India's agricultural land is cultivable.

8. Indian farmers still do farming using traditional methods.
9. To increase agricultural crop production, Indian farmers have been adopting since the 1960.
10. Irrigation is required in India due to irregular weather conditions.

REFERENCES:

1. Chauhan, Dharmendra Singh (2010): "Agricultural Geography", Ritu Publications Jaipur, India.
2. Gautam, Alka (2012): "Agricultural Geography", Sharda Pustak Bhavan Allahabad.
3. Husain, Majid (1996): "Systematic Agricultural Geography", Reprinted 2007, Rawat Publication, Jaipur and New Delhi.
4. Mamoria, Chaturbhuj. (1992): "Adhunik Bharat ka Brihat Bhoogol", Sahitya Bhavan, Agra.
5. Ojha, S.S. "Bharat ka Bhoogol". (2005): Bhaugolik Adhyan Sansthan, Govindpur, Allahabad.
6. Singh, J. and Dhillon, S.S. (2nd ed.). (2000): "Agricultural Geography", Tata McGraw Hill, New Delhi.
7. Tiwari, R.C. (2004): "Geography of India", Prayag Pustak Bhawan, Allahabad.
8. Agriculture Survey of India, 2017-18.
9. Economic Survey of India (vol.1st and 2nd). Oxford University Press, New Delhi.
10. Indian Budget, 2017-18.
11. Industrial Survey of India, 2107-18.
12. Khan, A. S. (1968): "Technological Change and Their Diffusion in Agriculture, Problem of Agriculture development in India", Edited by Dr. S. S. Jain, Kitab Mahal, Allahabad.
13. Khan, A. S. (1968): "Technological Change and Their Diffusion in Agriculture, Problem of Agriculture development in India", Edited by Dr. S. S. Jain, Kitab Mahal, Allahabad.
14. Lekhi, R. K. and Singh, Jogindar (2012): "Agricultural Economics", Kalyani Publishers, Ludhiana, New Delhi
15. Sharma, T. C. (1999): "Technological change In Indian Agriculture, A Regional Perspective", Rawat Publications, Jaipur and New Delhi

16. Singh, J. and Dhillon, S.S. (2nd ed.). (2000): "Agricultural Geography", Tata McGraw Hill, New Delhi.

17. Singh, Jasbir and Dhillon, S. S. (1984): "Agricultural Geography", Tata Mc Graw Hill publishing company Limited,

18. Singh, L.R. (ed.). (1987): "India: A Regional Geography", New Printindia Pvt. Ltd., Ghaziabad, U.P.

19. Symons, L. (1968): "Agriculture Geography". G. Bell and Sons Ltd. London.

20. Taylor, James A. (1968 ed.): "Weather and Agriculture", Oxford: Pergamon.

21. Young, Arthor. (1770): "Environment and Cropping Patterns in England".

TERMINAL QUESTIONS:

A. **Long Questions**

1. Define role of agriculture in Indian economy with its salient features?

2. What do you mean by agricultural infrastructure? Explain role of agricultural infrastructure in regional development?

3. Discuss the agricultural infrastructure and explain irrigation and its various methods in Indian context?

4. Explain the role of power, fertilizers and HYV seeds in agricultural development of India?

B. **Short Questions**

1. What is the significance of agricultural infrastructure development in India?

2. What are some key components of agricultural infrastructure in India?

3. How does the development of cold storage facilities impact India's agricultural sector?

4. What role does transportation infrastructure play in connecting rural farmers to markets in India?

5. How has technology been integrated into agricultural infrastructure development in recent years?
6. What challenges and obstacles does India face in enhancing agricultural infrastructure?
7. What potential benefits can be realized by improving agricultural infrastructure for Indian farmers and the overall economy?
8. Why is irrigation important for agriculture in India?
9. What are the major sources of irrigation in India?
10. What are some of the challenges and issues related to irrigation in India?
11. What is the significance of the Indira Gandhi Canal, and in which Indian state is it located?
12. Name the canal system that originates from the Sutlej River and plays a vital role in providing irrigation to northwestern states like Rajasthan and Haryana.

C. **Multiple Choice Questions**

1. What percentage of India's population is employed in the agricultural sector? a) 25%

a. 50%
b. 75%
c. 90%

(Answers: c)

2. Which of the following states in India is known as the "Rice Bowl of India"?

a. Punjab
b. Kerala
c. West Bengal
d. Rajasthan

(Answers: c)

3. Which crop is commonly referred to as the "Golden Fiber" in India?

a. Wheat
b. Cotton
c. Sugarcane
d. Pulses

(Answers: b)

4. What is the main source of irrigation in India?

a. Canals
b. Tube wells
c. Rainwater
d. Lakes and rivers

(Answers: a)

5. The Green Revolution in India primarily focused on increasing the production of which crop?

a. Rice
b. Wheat
c. Cotton
d. Sugarcane

(Answers: b)

6. Which agricultural practice is commonly followed in the arid and semi-arid regions of India to conserve soil moisture?

a. Organic farming
b. Crop rotation
c. Drip irrigation
d. Dryland farming

(Answers: d)

7. Which Indian state is known for its production of saffron, mainly grown in the region of Pampore?

a. Punjab
b. Jammu and Kashmir
c. Haryana
d. Himachal Pradesh

(Answers: b)

8. In India, the Kharif season refers to the:

a. Summer crop season
b. Winter crop season
c. Monsoon crop season
d. Rabi crop season

(Answers: c)

9. Which state in India is the largest producer of horticultural crops, including fruits and vegetables?

a. Maharashtra
b. Uttar Pradesh
c. Andhra Pradesh
d. Tamil Nadu

(Answers: a)

10. What is the main objective of the National Mission for Sustainable Agriculture (NMSA) in India?

a. Promoting organic farming
b. Enhancing farm mechanization
c. Increasing agricultural productivity and ensuring the sustainability of agriculture
d. Expanding agricultural credit facilities

(Answers: c)

D. Other Objective Type Questions:

1. How much percentage of population of India was engaged in agriculture during 1950-51?

2. Name four food crops of India?

3. How much percentage of cropped area in India is covered by food crops?

4. Sugarcane is which type of crop?

   a) Food crop b) Cash crop

5. Give examples of drinkable crops?

6. Name important factors determining agriculture in India?

7. What are HYV seeds?

8. How much percentage of India's land is available for farming?

9. Give examples of input based infrastructure in agriculture?

10. What irrigation means?

11. Indian agriculture is much depends on monsoonal rain-

    a) True b) False

12. Where Buckingham canal is used for irrigation?

13. Give examples of non-renewable energy resources?

14. What is the appropriate ratio of NPK for crops?

15. Where HYV of wheat was developed firstly in the world?

16. Which rice seed was found suitable in Indian geographical conditions?

    Answers to part (D):

1. 69.5%
2. 64.18%
3. Wheat, Rice, Maize, Gram
4. b) Cash crop
5. Tea, Coffee, Tobacco
6. Physical, Institutional and technological factors
7. Provide more production per hectare as compared to other seeds HYV- High Yielding variety seeds
8. 55%
9. Seeds, fertilizers, pesticides etc.
10. to supply water artificially to the crops
11. True
12. Andhra Pradesh and Tamil Nadu
13. Petroleum, Coal etc.
14. 4:2:1
15. Mexico
16. IR-8

CHAPTER SIX

INSTITUTIONAL FACTORS

INTRODUCTION:

Agriculture in India is influenced and determined by various physical, institutional and technological factors. Physical factors like topography, climate, and soils are important. Besides these, Institutional factors play a crucial role in influencing agriculture and crop production in India. These factors primarily encompass aspects such as land holding size, the land tenure system, and the implementation of land reforms. These elements collectively contribute significantly to shaping the agricultural landscape of the country.

The size of land holdings directly affects agricultural practices and productivity. In India, the distribution of land holdings among farmers varies widely, influencing the scale and efficiency of farming operations. Moreover, the tenure system, which defines how land is owned, leased, or managed, profoundly impacts agricultural decisions and investments. Secure land tenure encourages long-term investments in land improvement and technology adoption.

Additionally, land reforms, aimed at redistributing land ownership and improving access to land for marginalized groups, have historically played a pivotal role in transforming agricultural productivity. Reforms that ensure equitable distribution of land can enhance agricultural output by enabling more efficient land use and incentivizing investments in agricultural inputs.

Technological factors also significantly shape agriculture in India. Key technologies include irrigation systems, which ensure water availability during critical periods, thereby stabilizing crop yields. The adoption of high-yielding variety seeds has revolutionized crop production by increasing yields per unit of land. Similarly, the widespread use of chemical fertilizers has boosted soil fertility and crop productivity, although sustainable practices are increasingly emphasized.

Moreover, pesticides play a crucial role in protecting crops from pests and diseases, safeguarding yield and quality. Agricultural machinery, ranging from simple tools to advanced equipment, enhances efficiency in planting, cultivation, and harvesting operations, thereby reducing labor requirements and operational costs.

These technological factors collectively influence agricultural practices and productivity both independently and synergistically. Their adoption and effective use are critical determinants of crop production outcomes in India. By leveraging institutional reforms alongside appropriate technological advancements, Indian agriculture can achieve sustainable growth, ensure food security, and mitigate challenges posed by climate change and fluctuating market conditions.

INSTITUTIONAL FACTORS:

Besides physical factors, institutional factors are important determinant of agriculture. Growth and development of agriculture and agricultural production; quality and quantity of crops very much decided by these factors of land holding size, practiced traditions, land reforms and prevalent land tenure systems. Countries like India, where huge socio-economic imbalances are prevalent, and these factors play important role in agricultural development. Present agricultural status of India is the result of institutional factors prevalent as all these fix the field size, cropping pattern, crop types, land use, and crop productivity. Brief reviews of these institutional factors and their impacts as under:

LAND HOLDING PATTERN:

The term 'agricultural holding' designate average size of agricultural land held by the farmers in India. An operational land holding in India is a unit of land used wholly or partly for agricultural production and operated by one person alone or with the support of others members. An operational land holding may have of either only one or more packages of land. Operational land holdings include only those units which are used either in crop production or collectively for crop production with livestock and poultry products or other allied agricultural activities.

There are five kinds of land holdings in India, depending on various sizes, for instance, marginal holdings, small holdings, semi-medium, medium holdings, and large holdings; maximum number of operational land holdings in India is marginal holdings. The concept of agricultural operational holdings does not include those land holdings which are not operating any agricultural land and are engaged completely in livestock, poultry and fishing or others etc. On the basis of operated area, operational holdings by Agriculture Census are categorized as follows:

Sl. No.	Category	Operated Area
1.	Marginal holdings	< 1.00 hectare
2.	Small holdings	1.00 – 2.00 hectares
3.	Semi-Medium holdings	2.00 – 4.00 hectares
4.	Medium holdings	4.00 – 10.00 hectares
5.	Large holdings	10.00 hectares and above

Table 6.1: Categorization of Size of Holdings.

There are two concepts prevalent in India regarding land holdings; one is operational land holding and another one is ownership holding. Operational holding is the land, which is used for or under the agricultural activities; partially or fully. While ownership holding is the result of fragmentation of land holding with the time and not necessarily under agricultural use. In India land holding size is very small thus land is not much economically viable. Main cause of small land holding size is the continuously growing population of the country and faulty system of inheritance; making land holding size small to smaller with every generation. As in India father's land is divided into his sons (ownership by inheritance) results in decreased size of land holdings. Fragmentation of land is also the result of land inheritance system prevalent in India.

With the time size of land holdings decreased and number of holdings increased. In the year 1970-71 numbers of land holdings in India were about 71 million which increased to 115.6 million in 1995-96 i.e. number of land holdings increased by 62% while operational land holding increased only 1.1% i.e. from 162 million hectare to 163.48 million hectare in the same time span. According to one estimate per capita availability of agricultural land decreased from 0.29 hectare of 1971 to 0.13 hectare in 1991. The average size of land holdings also decreased from

2.28 hectare of 1970-71 to 1.41 hectare in 1995-96. All these are uneconomical for carrying agricultural operations beneficially. Owners of such a small size of land holdings with great fragmentation are not much sound economically and cannot bear the higher coasts of irrigation, fertilizers, pesticides, high yielding varicty seeds (HYV's seeds), and new farm machinery. Thus crop production and productivity suffer a lot.

For the planning purpose and accomplishment of land reforms, complete information about the characteristics of different size classes of land holdings is essential. This is also necessary to identify and devise programmes and policies for the benefits of small and marginal farmers especially, the rural poor and economically weaker sections of the society. The information is required by operational holdings as distinct from ownership holdings. An operational holding is defined as 'all land, which is used wholly or partly for agricultural production and is operated as one technical unit by one person alone or with others without regard to title, legal form, size or location'. Thus, the Agricultural Census of operational holdings assumes importance as a source of basic data required for several uses. Out of the total number of 97.8 million holding in 1985-86, 58.1 per cent was of marginal category, and the remaining were the categories of holding include small category (18.3 per cent), semi-medium (13.6 per cent), medium (8.1 per cent) and large (2.0 per cent).

According to the Census data of 2010-11, about 67 percent of India's agricultural land is detained by the marginal farmers having land holding size below one hectare and 18 per cent were classified as small (one-two hectare). Whereas, it is estimated that only 0.7% percent agricultural land is under large holdings of 10 hectares and above. The average size of the holding has been estimated as 1.15 hectares. The average size of land holdings is showing a sturdy declining trend over various Agriculture Censuses since 1970-71. This evidently shows the strain that marginal farmers experience in India.

As per the Agriculture Census 2010-11, total number of operational holdings was estimated to as 138.35 million. The total operated area was 159.59 million hectares. The number of agricultural operational holdings in the country has seen a steady increase over the years. From 115.58 million operational holdings in 1995-96, this number has increased to 138.35 million operational holdings in 2010-11, an increase of 20% over 16 years. The total operated area has seen mixed trend. It reduced from 163.35 million hectares in 1995-96 to 158.32 million hectares in 2005-06. In 2010-11, it increased to 159.59 million hectares. The average size of land holding has been continuously decreasing on account of increasing number of land holdings from an average of 1.41 hectares in 1995-96. It went down to 1.15 hectares in 2010-11, a decrease of percent.

The percentage of marginal holdings has gone up from 62.9% in 2000-01 to 67.1% in 2010-11. Except the percentage of marginal holdings, the percentage of all other holdings has gone down marginally from 2000-01 to 2010-11. The percentage of large holdings has gone down from 1% in 2000-01 to 0.7% in 2010-11. The percentage of medium holdings went down from 5.3% in 2000-01 to 4.3% in 2010-11.

Following the trends of percentage of land holdings, the percentage of area operated increased for marginal holdings and decreased for all other categories except small holdings. Surprisingly, though the percentage of small land holdings has gone down from 18.9% in 2000- 01 to 17.9% in 2010-11, the percentage area under small land holdings increased from 20.2% in 2000-01 to 22.08% in 2010-11. This could be probably because of the increase in total area under operation. The percentage area under marginal land holdings increased from 18.7% in 2000-01 to 22.5% in 2010-11. While the number of medium and large land holdings account for less than 5%, they make up for close to $1/3^{rd}$ of the total area under operation. Though the number of marginal & small holdings account for 85% of the total number of holdings, they together account for only 45% of the total area under operation.

TENURE SYSTEMS:

Land tenure specifically refers to the system in which land is held by an individual from the Government. It shows the relationships between the land holder and the State and supreme possession of land rests with the Government. Government gives proprietary rights to the individuals or communities. Thus, a land owner is in that sense is only a proprietor of that land and he has to pay land revenue for that. Land is held all over the world under different tenure situations. Holding of land depends on different reasons. Ownership or exclusive control by an individual is not the only concept under which land is held and used. If we look from Indian point of view, ownership of land is a western idea. In our country, ownership of land, before the Permanent Land Settlement, always rested with the community. However, in western world, individual ownership of land was recognized both by the state and the community.

In ancient times, the state claimed a share of the produce of the land from the farmer. The laws of *Manu* mentioned one sixth as the legal share of the King of the gross crop produce but during the war and various other emergencies, it was increased to one fourth. It was *Timur* who represented the first systematic attempt in the direction of converting the State's share of the crop produce into money. *Sher-shah Suri* made some improvement in his short reign. The most famous arrangement of land revenue was made under Akbar by his Finance Minister, *Todarmal*; in that time fixation of land revenue; systematic and complete investigation was made to assess the taxable capacity of different lands. Then agricultural land was carefully measured and divided into four classes representing different grades of fertility.

Maratha rulers continued the same system and fixed `Kamal' or the maximum rates for the best lands. The assessment was not permanent in majority of the cases. Later 'revenue farmer' came into existence who paid the Government nine-tenth of the whole collection and kept the rest as his collection charges, after that the right of collecting land revenue started for a pargana or a district and they were sold by public auction to the highest bidders. Due to this, the great exploitation of the farmers started. The revenue farmers became more dominant. This revenue farming system which started during the *Mughal* rule in Bengal was soon extended to the other parts of the country. In United Provinces and Punjab revenue farmers succeeded to gain certain aristocratic rights. The distortions and disorders in the revenue system resulted in many complexities of land tenures and rights. Under British Rule, there three main land tenure systems were prevalent in India. They were *Zamindari, Mahalwari* and *Rayatwari*.

Zamindari:

This system in India was introduced by Lord Cornwallis in Bengal in 1793. He got a particular percentage of the land revenue collected from the farmers. Under this system, the land of the village or few villages was held by one person or few joint owners who were responsible for payment of land revenue to the Government. These middle men or the land lord grasp land revenue from the small farmers and pay it to the Government. There used to be number of intermediaries between the Zamindars and the actual tillers of the soil. The system later acquired various forms such as Zamindari, Jagirdari, Inamdari, etc. In this system of land tenure farmers do not have direct relation with the Government thus they are subjected to all sorts of exploitation. This system was prevalent in Bihar, Uttar Pradesh, Orissa and state of Madras. This system of land tenure had various qualities as well as drawbacks. This system worked well where the Zamindars were educated and feels the importance of the land reform and improvement in agriculture. This system did not worked well where the Zamindars were interested only in collecting land revenue.

Mahalwari:

In this type of land tenure system, not only the single person or the Zamindar was responsible for payment of the land revenue to the government but other farmers of the village were also responsible for it. Residents of a village were collectively and sincerely responsible for payment of the revenue. In such a type of land tenure there was also a head of various Zamindars, here also the farmers did not have direct links with the Government. This type of system was prevalent in Uttar Pradesh, Madhya Pradesh, and Punjab etc.

In this system, common farmers were not happy. They suffered from exploitation and also many other drawbacks were incorporated in this system. In this system land lords who were known as 'Mahalbords' had full control over the internal arrangement and so they exploited farmers as by imposing faulty rules of revenue collection. In this system, the rights of the village lands were held jointly by the village communities, the members of which were jointly and severally responsible for the payment of the land revenue. Land revenue was fixed for the whole village and the village headman called as *Lumberdar* collected it, for which he received 'Panchatra' i.e. 5 per cent as commission.

Rayatwari:

In this type of land tenure system, the property rights of the land vested on the Government; farmers paid the revenue to the Government, for cultivation on that land so long as the farmer paid the revenue, he could not be rejected from the land. Previously, this system was prevalent in Madhya Pradesh, Bombay, Assam etc. but latter spread in almost all the states where Zamindari and Mahalbari system have been abolished. This is the only system of land tenure in which farmers have the direct relationships with the Government. It was also helpful for the Government as when the land increases the revenue also increases. The farmers also have right over the land so that they were interested in improving and making it useful and more economic.

This system was controlled by the Government employees and they create trouble to the farmers so many times. Firstly system was introduced by *Sir Thomas Munro* in 1820 in the Madras State and after that in Bombay State. Every registered land holder was recognized as proprietor and he could sell or transfer the land rights to others. It was a better system as compared to Zamindari or Mahalwari and various other forms of tenure.

CONSOLIDATION SETUP:

Agriculture Census in India is conducted at the interval of five years for collection of information/data about the structural aspects of farm holdings in the country. The basic unit for data is the area under operational holding. In general Agriculture Census data is collected in three phases - first on primary subjects like the numbers and area of operational holdings, then a detailed survey based on samples from 20 percent of villages on tenancy, land use, irrigation and finally on the patterns of input use in agricultural production. In India land holding size is very small on an average of 1.15 hectares as compared to land holding of USA (158 hectares) and Canada (1993 hectare) but bigger than the land holding size of Japan which is only one hectare. Main culprit of small size of land holding in India are continuously increasing population, low of inheritance, fragmentation of joint families, rural debts and decline of craft and cottage industries. Small land holdings are not beneficial for the use of modern tools and techniques, diffusion of HYV seeds, fertilizers, etc. and also not economically viable, wastage of land is at the peak. All these problems can be reduced by adopting the proper land consolidation methods. In India land consolidation mainly done by the government but consciousness and awareness of farmers is also important in this regard.

Land consolidation pragramme was implemented successfully in the states like Punjab, Haryana and Madhya Pradesh. Various efforts are taken to successfully implement this programme in Bihar and Jammu and Kashmir. But at latest only 49% agricultural land has been consolidated and remaining 51% is still waiting for land consolidation in the country effecting agricultural production a lot.

LAND REFORMS:

Land reform is a broad term, refers to the reforms of institutional factors related to land in order to promote the agricultural production and also to raise the level of income and standard of living of the farmers in India or it refers to an institutional measure directed towards changing the existing pattern of land ownership; tenancy rights and management of land. Institutional factors along with technical factors play an important role in agricultural production. These institutional factors include land tenure system, land holdings size; farming structure, land distribution, intermediaries present etc.

Major land reform measures have been introduced time to time by various underdeveloped and developing countries in the world for achieving a rational land distribution pattern and feasible farming structure. In most of the underdeveloped countries land reforms are among one of the main foundation stone of agrarian policy. The term 'land reforms' encompasses two different meaning; in a narrow sense, land reforms are concerned with the reforms related to land ownership and land holdings.

But in a broader sense, the term 'land reforms' is used to mean those measures of reforms necessary to raise production of crops by increasing agricultural productivity; include reforms concerning to rent fixation on land, abolition of intermediaries, credit and marketing arrangements, etc. In order to attain institutional changes in agriculture land reforms are considered effective. Prof. Gunner Myrdal argued, in this connection, that the "Land reforms are a planned and institutional reorganization of the relation between man and land."

Although, agriculture is the main occupation of population in India, yet it is backward. Agricultural productivity in India is still very low as compared to other countries of the world. At the time of independence, there were many unfair systems of land tenure were in action that deprived a large number of farmers throughout the country. The ownership rights were faulty. There was Zamindari system prevalent in India. The farmers own very small and limited pieces of land which was not viable socially and economically.

The problems of fragmentation and uneconomic holdings were resulting into low crop productivity. The institutional factors like-the feudal structure of society, the small size of land holdings, the presence of Zamindars or intermediaries, high land rents and insecurity of tenancy rights led to the backwardness of society and agriculture too. After independence, country felt the greater needs of the land reforms to heal the socio-economic structure of rural India and to stop exploitation of the genuine tilters of the land and pass on the ownership rights to them.

The major objectives of land reform in India were as follows:

1. Restructuring the faulty agrarian structure to achieve democratic structure
2. Abolition of intermediaries
3. Land consolidation measures and check land fragmentations
4. Land ceiling
5. Elimination of exploitation of farmers and actual land tillers
6. Actualization of the goal of 'land to the tiller'
7. Improvement of socio-economic conditions of the rural poor by extending their land base
8. Increasing agricultural production and productivity
9. Facilitating land-based development of rural poor
10. Achieve the goals of sustainable growth and social justice

Measures of Land Reforms in India:

Abolition of intermediaries:

At the time of independence, different intermediaries like Zamindars, Talukdars, Jagirdars and Inams were dominated the agricultural sector in India. Thus the top priority of the then government was abolition of these intermediary tenures. Soon after the independence, measures for the abolition of the Zamindari system were adopted in different states of India. The first Act to abolish intermediaries was passed in 1948 in Madras state. Since then, state after state passed legislation to abolish the Zamindari rights.

In 1951 Orissa Estates Abolition Act was passed. By the year 1955, the progress for the abolition of intermediaries had been completed in almost all the states of India. As a result of these measures, about 2.5 crore farmers were brought into direct relationship with the State and facilitated distribution of about 61 lakh hectares of land to the landless farmers. Large areas of privately-owned forests and wasteland now were under the ownership of the State. Despite the abolition of intermediaries at a large scale, poor farmers were continued to be exploited in various ways thus a large-scale of poor tenants leave the agriculture. While land lordship has been abolished but absentee land lordships were continues to flourish.

All this happened because the law permitted the intermediaries to retain their home farms, no limits were put on the area of land they could retain, the term 'personal cultivation' was nonspecific i.e. poorly defined and proper protection was not given to actual tenants. Undoubtedly, this abolition of intermediaries paved the way for an outstanding move regarding agricultural reforms in India but the goal of "land to the tiller" is yet to be achieved.

Tenancy Reforms:

Land tenancy refers to the relation between the land holder i.e. land owner and the actual tiller of the land. Many land owners did not cultivate their lands personally but gave it to some other tiller and receive rent for that land called as 'absentee landlords'. Tenancy legislations have three steps for instance, regulation of rent, providing security of tenure, and give rights of land ownership to the tenants.

According to the rules rent payable to the landowners should not exceed one-fifth to one- fourth of the gross produce of land in any condition; but large inter-state variations are widespread in actual fixation of land rent rates. Tenancy legislations have made it clear that in no case the tenants can be expelled except only in the situation where landlords themselves want to continue agriculture. Even in the event of resumption of cultivation by the owners, tenancy legislations have made it obligatory to leave a minimum area for the tenant. But overall impact of tenancy reforms is very limited.

Firstly, tenancy laws have been violated all around the country. For instance, in Bihar and Uttar Pradesh, the maximum limit of rent was at 25 % of the gross produce but tenants are paying 50% or more of gross produce due to various social conditions. The tenants are exploited by the land owners by way of heavy rents (50 per cent or even $2/3^{rd}$ of the produce). There are no protections of tenure and there are no any incentives have been provided to the tenants to make land enhancement and increase production.

Ceiling on land holdings:

Second five year plan (1956-1961) recommended the obligation of ceilings on agricultural holdings to reduce the existing disparities in the pattern of land-ownership and make some land available for distribution to the landless agricultural laborers. It was visualized and fixed that land above a certain fixed limit would be acquired by the State and redistributed among the landless laborers and to the small farmers, to create economically viable land holdings in all the states.

There were two phases in the land ceiling laws. In the first phase 'landholder' was treated as the unit of the farming but in second phase after 1972 it was changed to 'family' and ceiling limits were lowered. But exclusion of orchards, sugarcane plantations, grazing lands, cattle- breeding farms, religious, charitable and educational trusts, tanks, and fisheries etc. have made the ceiling laws almost disused. Total amount of land declared surplus was 73.67 lakh acres in September 2001 and about 64.95 lakh acres of land have been taken over by the states and 53.79 lakh acres of land have been distributed among 54.84 lakh tenants in the country.

About 12 lakh acres of land could not be distributed due to variety of reasons. The operations of the ceiling law made virtually no impact on the agrarian structure. The enforcement of the ceiling law delayed for several years which enabled landowners to manipulate land records at a large leading to fictitious (benami) and fraudulent partitions of lands among their relatives, friends, fictitious trusts, etc. Mainly due to a wide range of exemptions provided in the ceiling laws, various shortcomings and loopholes in the laws and ineffective implementations of the laws ceiling of land holdings actually failed leaving some small landowners who were caught in the net and most of the big landowners were escaped. Land was not acquired and was not redistributed among the landless peasants leaving some exceptions. Lack of political willing can be considered as the greatest hindrance in the speedy implementation, acquisition and redistribution of land to the land less laborers and small farmers in India.

Consolidation of land holdings:

Fragmented, separated and erratic land holdings with very small size have made Indian agriculture totally unrealistic, unsustainable and unprofitable. Consolidations of these fragmented and small sized farms are necessary to improve the efficiency and economic viability of agriculture in India and raise the living standards of rural population and farmers. Land consolidations have been completed in the states of Punjab, Uttar Pradesh and Haryana in India till 2001. Very less area, about 163.3 lakh acres (1/3rd of the total cultivated area) in India have been consolidated so the success story of land consolidations is rather disappointing. Small farmers have a strong fear that consolidation favors large farmers; they don't want to avail land consolidation measures due different social and economic problems also.

70 years after independence, land reforms in India are not fully implemented. There are huge ambiguities in the land reform laws and their

implementation is also defective. Poor governmental implementation mechanism, corrupt bureaucrats, and officials etc. are the main culprit of failure to land consolidation measures in India.

Co-operative farming:

Co-operative farming has been promoted to solve the problems of frequent small sized and fragmented holdings in India. In this system, farmers pool their small sized land holdings for farming and reap the benefits of large scale farming with the help of co-operatives. It is a type of group farming dome in co-operation. Thus the advantages of technical farming, HYV seeds and adequate use of irrigation and fertilizers can be gained by the co-operative farms and farmers; co-operative farming lays the base of strong democratic sense, self and mutual help. But in India co-operative farming is not in strong position due to different social structure, likes and dislikes, and prejudice of the India population. Co-operative farming in India has largely been a failure. The attitude of the bureaucrats and of the Indian farmers towards the co-operative farming is not much positive.

Bhoodan Movement:

Acharya Vinoba Bhabe was the precursor of the 'Bhoodan Movement' in India. In this movement he collected land from the rich landlords and distributed that land to the landless peoples. About 4.2 million acres of land were received as 'Bhoodan', but so far only about 1.3 million acres have been distributed among landless population. Presently this movement is in the demise.

Compilation and updating of land records:

Collection and renewal of the land records are prerequisite and an essential condition for the successful and well-organized implementation of land reform programmes. In recent time in India the states have been advocated to take all measures for updating land records with the highest urgency by adopting a time-bound programme. Efforts are also being made to maintain the land records in digital forms with the help of computers, scanners and digitizers; in this regard GIS (Geographical Information System) is an important tool for land record up gradation, preservation and management.

Causes of failure of land reforms in India:

There are a number of causes for the failure of the land reforms programmes in India.

Among them some important ones are as follows:

1. **Unnecessary publicity and delay in passing land reform laws:** Much publicity of the proposed land reforms and the time taken for a bill to become an Act in many states has been unusually long. This has enabled the landowners to make essential alterations in the provisions of land reform legislations.

2. **Ambiguous definitions of various terms:** Various terms related with the land reforms are not well explained thus chances of miss interpretations are huge. For example the term 'Personal cultivation' is relatively loose. One could recommence land for personal cultivation easily under the definition living very distant from the land. The Zamindars have been permitted to hold large areas of land for agriculture. The land reform laws have provided immunity to the land awarded for bravery, land under orchards and sugarcane, tea estates, efficient farms, trusts, educational, and religious land etc.

3. **Optional nature of the laws:** Most of the land reform laws which grant ownership rights to the tenants are not mandatory rather are optional. The tenants have to go to the government offices for grant of ownership rights on land. They will not get them automatically. On many occasions, tenants hesitate to approach the courts for this purpose just only due to fear of the rich landlords and corrupt official.

- **Malafide transfer of land:** To cheat and defeat the noble cause of land ceiling and laws relating to land ceilings, the Zamindars and landlords have indulged in large scale transfer of land to their family members, relatives, and friends. Due to such faulty practices no real changes has been felt in the operational agriculture scenario.

- **Lack of social consciousness among the tenants:** Social consciousness of the tenants is a major factor responsible for the successful implementation of land reforms in India. Due to lack of awareness and consciousness of the farmers goals of land reforms, land consolidation and land ceiling have been not achieved yet. Everyone has to fight for his rights and those farmers too.

- **State takes side of the big farmers:** It can be witnessed in many cases that state plans and policies favors big farmers and landlords rather small farmers so that the interests of the small farmers have been critically affected.

- **Lack of political willpower:** The programme of land reforms requires adequate political wish, enthusiasm and support at all stages of land reforms whether it is the case of law and act formation or implementation. But unfortunately the political leaders wear a mask of progressive socialistic attitude they only do the politics not the reforms, the lack of political will is fully demonstrated by the large gaps between policy and legislation and between law and its implementation in reality.

- **Bureaucratic corruption:** Land reforms implementation provides a golden opportunity to the 'Patwari' and other revenue officials and functionaries of the Revenue Department to make easy money. In many cases the highly placed officials in the revenue and administrative departments are themselves landlords. Some honest officials implement the laws of land reforms sincerely, but they face unnecessary difficulties and problems from landlords and politicians of our country.

- **Surplus land is fallow and uncultivable land:** The land holders of surplus land manipulate the land data in such a way that the land in excess in their possession is usually barren and uncultivable. Such a surplus land does not yield any benefit to the landless peasants. In this way the very purpose of land reforms legislation is defeated.

- **Absence of records:** Absence of land records regarding ownership and possession in India is a common case.

- **Lack of uniformity in land reforms laws:** Land reforms laws are not uniform throughout the Indian states. Different laws among various Indian states, accounts for the slow development of land reforms measures in the country.

SUMMARY:

Various institutional factors like land holdings; size and fragmentation, land tenancy, and land reforms are importantly fix the agricultural production and productivity in India and the links of farmers to the land. In India most of the farmers hold marginal land holdings with fragmented farms, tenancy is also very faulty and various traces of land-lordships, zamindari, mahalwari and rayatwari (ryotwari), lumberdari systems etc. can be seen throughout the Indian states. Land reforms are saying the story of failures; farmers are leaving agriculture and seeking jobs in cities. All these are big hindrances in the agricultural growth and development and use of modern tools, techniques and innovations in agriculture in India. Shares of agricultural in employment generation and GDP are decreasing continuously.

A number of land reforms have been implemented time to time in India but they are not providing fruitful results till date. Agriculture is not a viable economic activity for most of the farmers in India as most of them are of small and marginal. Farmers can't use highly developed tools and techniques, HYV seeds and chemical fertilizers due to prevalent social and economic constraints. Various remedial measures have been made to remove the difficulties and structural constraints pertaining to land reforms in India. India is characterized by a tradition of inequality and exploitation of the poor farmers all the ages, the land reform measures can lead to a real burst of enthusiasm, a genuine release of energy among the farmers and crop production and productivity can be raised many times.

Needs of the present is the proper implementation of land reforms. In order to remove hindrances prevalent in agricultural institutions in India the poor should be motivated through education and extension services and the rich should be compelled to cooperate through compulsion. It certainly requires a government with strong political spirit and bureaucracy which is committed to achieve the desired land reforms results.

To cope up with these problems and to increase the viability of agriculture among farmers efficient formulation and implementation of land reforms are must. Government with strong will power can do the miracle. People's participation, education, research and innovations are required for making agriculture more economic so that the living standards of the poor farmers can be raised.

GLOSSARY:

1. **HYV-** High Yielding Variety
2. **GDP-** Gross Domestic Produce
3. **Bhoodan-** donation of land
4. **Co-operative-** an autonomous association of persons united to meet common social, economic and cultural goals
5. **Land holding-** land owned or rented
6. **Tennant-** one who has temporary possession of land
7. **Ceiling-** fixing maximum size of land holding
8. **Consolidation-** combining a number of things into one
9. **Inheritance-** practice of passing property to the descendants

10. **Reforms**- make change in order to improve

CHECK YOUR PROGRESS:

1. Factors relating to, or managed and formulated by an institution are known as institutional factors.
2. Land holding size, practiced traditions, land reforms and prevalent land tenure systems are the major components of Institutional factors.
3. The term 'agricultural holding' designate average size of agricultural land held by the farmers in India
4. operational land holding in India is a unit of land used wholly or partly for agricultural production and operated by one person alone or with the support of others members
5. 1.41 hectare was the average size of land holding in India in 1995-96.
6. 67 percent of agricultural land was detained by the marginal farmers in 2010-11.
7. Land tenancy refers to the system in which land is held by an individual from government
8. Three tenure systems were prevalent in India during the British rule.
9. Zamindari, Mahalwari, and Rayatwari were the name of tenure systems in British rule.
10. Lord Cornwallis in 1793 introduced the Zamindari system in India.
11. Sir Thomas Munro in Madras state introduced the Rayatwari system in India.
12. Maximum limit of land one can retain is land ceiling.
13. A type of group farming in co-operation is Co-operative farming.
14. Acharya Vinoba Bhabe was the initiator of Bhoodan movement.

REFERENCES:

1. Chauhan, Dharmendra Singh (2010): "Agricultural Geography", Ritu Publications Jaipur, India.
2. Gautam, Alka (2012): "Agricultural Geography", Sharda Pustak Bhavan Allahabad.

3. Husain, Majid (1996): "Systematic Agricultural Geography", Reprinted 2007, Rawat Publication, Jaipur and New Delhi.

4. Mamoria, Chaturbhuj. (1992): "Adhunik Bharat ka Brihat Bhoogol", Sahitya Bhavan, Agra.

5. Ojha, S.S. "Bharat ka Bhoogol". (2005): Bhaugolik Adhyan Sansthan, Govindpur, Allahabad.

6. Singh, J. and Dhillon, S.S. (2nd ed.). (2000): "Agricultural Geography", Tata McGraw Hill, New Delhi.

7. Tiwari, R.C. (2004): "Geography of India", Prayag Pustak Bhawan, Allahabad.

8. Agriculture Survey of India, 2017-18.

9. Economic Survey of India (vol.1st and 2nd). Oxford University Press, New Delhi.

10. Indian Budget, 2017-18.

11. Industrial Survey of India, 2107-18.

12. Khan, A. S. (1968): "Technological Change and Their Diffusion in Agriculture, Problem of Agriculture development in India", Edited by Dr. S. S. Jain, Kitab Mahal, Alahabad.

13. Khan, A. S. (1968): "Technological Change and Their Diffusion in Agriculture, Problem of Agriculture development in India", Edited by Dr. S. S. Jain, Kitab Mahal, Alahabad.

14. Lekhi, R. K. and Singh, Jogindar (2012): "Agricultural Economics", kalyani Publishers, Ludhiana, New Delhi

15. Sharma, T. C. (1999): "Technological change In Indian Agriculture. A Regional Perspective", Rawat Publications, Jaipur and New Delhi

16. Singh, J. and Dhillon, S.S. (2nd ed.). (2000): "Agricultural Geography", Tata McGraw Hill, New Delhi.

17. Singh, Jasbir and Dhillon, S. S. (1984): "Agricultural Geography", Tata Mc Graw Hill publishing company Limited,

18. Singh, L.R. (ed.). (1987): "India: A Regional Geography", New Printindia Pvt. Ltd., Ghaziabad, U.P.

19. Symons, L. (1968): "Agriculture Geography", G. Bell and Sons Ltd. London.

20. Taylor, James A. (1968 ed.): "Weather and Agriculture", Oxford: Pergamon.

21. Young, Arthor. (1770): "Environment and Cropping Patterns in England".

TERMINAL QUESTIONS:

A. LONG QUESTIONS

1. Define the institutional factors and their role in agricultural development in India?
2. What do you mean by land reforms? Elaborate the important land reforms done in India?
3. What are the major objectives of the land reforms and also discuss the various causes responsible for failure of land reforms in India?

B. SHORT QUESTIONS

1. What is the meaning of institutional factors?
2. Write major components of institutional factors?
3. Define agricultural land holding?
4. What do you understand by operational holding?
5. What was the average size of land holding in India in 1995-96?
6. What percentage of agricultural land detained by marginal farmers in India in the year 2010- 11?
7. What do you mean by land tenancy?
8. How many tenure systems were prevalent in India during British rule?
9. Name the tenure systems during British rule?
10. Who introduced the zamindari system in India and when?
11. Who introduced the rayatwari system in India and where?
12. Define the term land ceiling?
13. What is co-operative farming?
14. Who was the initiator of Bhoodan Movement?

C. MULTIPLE CHOICE QUESTIONS

Q- 1 Meaning of agricultural holding?

1. Agricultural land size determined by the government.
2. Cultivable land area.
3. Non Agricultural land management.

4. None of the above.

(Answer- 1)

2. Where is Pollarding done?

1. Animal Husbandry Unit
2. Poultry Production Unit
3. Crop Production Unit
4. All of the above

(Answer - 4)

3. What is the number of agricultural holdings in India?

1. One
2. Two
3. Three
4. Five

(Answer- 4)

4. What is the size of the marginal landholding?

1. Below 1 hectare
2. 2 hectares
3. 3 to 4 hectares
4. 4 to 10 hectares

(Answer-1)

5. In what total area is marginal land operated in India?

1. 50%
2. 40%
3. 45%
4. 55%

(Answer- 3)

6. Who started the Zamindari system in India?

1. Lord Ripon
2. Lord Karnvalish
3. Lord macaulay
4. None of the above

(Answer- 2)

7. Who had the rights on the land in the Rayatwari system?

1. Public
2. Government
3. NGO
4. None of the above

(Answer-2)
8. Intent of land reform.

1. To consolidate
2. To provide l chemical fertilizers to farmers.
3. To increase agricultural production.
4. All of the above

(Answer- 3)

9. The main objectives of land reforms in India are?

1. To consolidate.
2. Increase agricultural crop production
3. Abolition of intermediaries
4. All of above

(Answer- 4)

10. How many stages are there in tenancy reform

1. 2
2. 3
3. 5
4. 8

(Answer-3)

CHAPTER SEVEN

INDUSTRIAL SCENARIO

INTRODUCTION:

Industry refers to an economic activity, concerned with the production of goods, extraction of minerals and to provide the services to the population for instance, iron and steel, cement, food processing and textile industries are related with the production of goods, coal mining industry linked with the extraction of coal and banking, health, education, entertainment and tourism industries are service providers.

Industries cannot be established just anywhere; they require specific prerequisites and amenities. Key factors influencing their location include the availability of raw materials, sufficient land, adequate water supply, affordable skilled and unskilled labour, reliable power sources, and access to capital, efficient transportation networks, and a market for their products. Industries tend to settle where one or more of these factors are readily accessible. The government plays a crucial role by providing essential infrastructure and incentives such as subsidized power and reduced transportation costs, encouraging industries to establish themselves in less developed areas.

The establishment of industries often catalyses the development of both the immediate vicinity and surrounding areas. This development typically extends to agriculture, trade, commerce, and the overall diversification of the economy and services in the region.

TYPES OF INDUSTRY:

In general industries can be classified in multiple as on the basis of type of raw materials used, their size and ownership of industry, or nature of produce etc. various types of industries are as follows:

1. **Raw material based industries:**

These industries are defined by the type of raw material used in them. These further may be classified as agro-based, mineral based, marine based and forest based industries depending upon the type of raw materials used in them. Agro-based industries use agriculture based products as their raw materials for instance sugarcane, food processing, vegetable oil, cotton and jute textile, rice and flour mills, dairy products and leather industries are the examples of agro- based industries. Mineral based industries are those use mineral ores as their raw materials. The products of these industries provide base to the other industries.

For example iron ore is the product of mineral based industry provides base to iron and steel industry. Aquatic/ marine based industries use products from the sea and oceans as their raw materials. Industries processing sea food and manufacturing cod liver oil are some examples of marine based industries. On the other side forest based industries utilize the raw materials from forests and process them into valuable products. The industries associated with forests are paper and pulp, pharmaceuticals, honey, lac, varnish and paint, furniture and buildings materials etc.

1. **Industries according to their size:**

Based on the size, industries can be classified into two group small scale and large scale industries. These industries count the amount of capital invested, number of people employed and the volume of production by them. Cottage or household industries are a subtype of small scale industries where products are manufactured by hand or very less mechanization, by the craftsmen in their homes without or very limited use of power sources. For instance pottery, various handicrafts, and basket weaving etc. are the examples of cottage industry or house hold industries. Small scale industries are those who use lesser amount of money and mechanization, lesser labours and lesser production as compared to large scale industries that produce huge volumes of products. Investments of capital are higher and the technology used is of superior quality in large scale industries. Silk weaving and food processing industries are the examples of small scale industries whereas production of automobiles, cement, ship manufacturing and heavy machinery like tractors, harvesters, etc. are large scale industries.

3. **Industries according to ownership:**

According to ownership rights industries can be classified into various sub-categories like private sector, state owned/public sector, joint/mixed sector and co-operative sector. Private sector industries primarily owned and operated by individuals or a group of individuals. The public sector industries are owned and operated by the state/government. Joint/mixed sector industries are owned and operated jointly by the state and individuals or a group of individuals while co-operative sector industries are owned and operated by the group of peoples like Amul etc.

Mineral based industry (Iron and Steel, Aluminum Industry, Cement Industry)

IRON AND STEEL INDUSTRY:

Being a developing country, Iron and Steel Industry has a very important role to play in India's future developments. The production of steel is regarded as one of the key feature and prerequisite for modern industrial development. Iron and steel industry is the basic industry of India. Speedy growth, development and industrialization of the country requires rapid development of iron and steel industries as they make available to the base to the development of other industries in the country. Development of agriculture, transportation and communication facilities, machine and tools making industry, electrical and electronics, machinery producing industry, consumer goods and service industry, and many more; are all depend on the development and expansion of iron and steel industries of the country. The development of iron and steel industry in India can be traced from very ancient times and for instance, can be witnessed by the iron beam of the Konark Temple of Orissa and the 7 meters high iron pillar near Qutab Minar in Delhi. Actual foundation of large scale production of iron and steel through modernized methods was started with the establishment of Tata Iron and Steel Company (TISCO) by Jamshed Ji Tata since 1907. Indian

Iron and Steel Company (IISCO) was established in Burnpur near Asansol in 1919. In 1923 Mysore Iron and Steel Company was established in private sector near Bhadrawati in Karnataka; presently it is known as Visvesvaraya Iron and Steel Works Ltd. In the second Five Year Plan (1956-61) government has established Hindustan Steel Limited and four other industries were established with the help of foreign located in Rourkela, Bhilai, Durgapur and Bokaro.

All the raw material used in iron and steel industry are heavy and weight loosing nature thus this industry can't get locate anywhere. The raw materials for iron & steel industry include iron ore, fuels like coal and coke, limestone, dolomite, silica, manganese, nickel, tungsten, etc. are also used in this industry. These industries also need plenty of water and electricity. Recycling of scrap matter to produce new steel is also very common. Iron and steel industry preferably are located near the sources of raw materials.

Later on, since the introduction of Fourth Plan, steps was also taken for the development of three more steel plants one each at Salem, Vijaynagar and Visakhapatnam. In 1974, the Steel Authority of India Limited (SAIL) was created for the development of steel industry, for supplying major inputs to the industry and also to bring a coordinated and synchronized development of all the major industrial units under its control. Major units were: Hindustan Steel Limited, Salem Steel Limited, Hindustan Steel Works Construction Limited, Bharat Coking Coal Limited and National Mineral Development Corporation Limited. The management of TISCO is also undertaken by SAIL. The SAIL is at present an integrated steel company with five public sector steel plants. At present about 70 per cent of domestic steel requirement is only met by SAIL. The steel industry is providing direct employment to more than 4 lakh workers. With crude steel production of 81.2 million metric tons, India is ranked as the fourth largest steel producing country in the world.

But, India is still lacking in of production of steel. Thus, a large gap between the consumption and production of steel still persists in domestic fronts. To meet this gap India is to import steel every year.

Problems of Iron and Steel Industry:
The iron and steel industry of the country is facing various problems. Major problems of iron and steel industry in India are-

1. Steel companies are overwhelmed with huge debts
2. Lack of domestic demand of higher grade steel

3. Low quality of metallurgical coke for blast furnace iron making
4. High input costs
5. Cheap imports from China, Korea and other countries are also a matter of concern for domestic producers
6. Inadequate supply of power and coal
7. Inefficiency of public sector units
8. Under-utilization of capacity
9. Lack of finance
10. Lack of technically trained workers
11. Sickness of mini steel plants
12. Problem of administrations
13. Increasing demand of iron and steel in recent years
14. Higher dependency on foreign investment
15. Problem of transportation for carrying raw materials and processed goods
16. Industrial disputes
17. Excess staff
18. Large demand and supply gap
19. Increasing global competition
20. Rise of cost of inputs continuously
21. Environmental concerns

Suggestions to solve the problems of iron and steel industry:

1. Improvement and up gradation of technologies,
2. Arrangement for the supply of best quality coal,
3. Full utilization of its capacity,
4. Diversification of production,
5. Adoption of efficient management of public sector steel units,
6. Solution of labour disputes,
7. Arrangement for proper training of workers,
8. Development of small factories,
9. Attaining stability in the increasing prices of the steel.
10. Liberalization of Steel Policy
11. Advancement of old machinery
12. Adequate and easy capital arrangements

In order to face these problems, the iron and steel industry needed a comprehensive planning for modernization, up gradation of technologies, replacement of obsolete equipment and removal of technological imbalances.

ALUMINIUM INDUSTRY:

Aluminum industry is the second largest metal industry of India after iron and steel industry. Aluminum is also the 3rd frequently available element present in the earth's crust and the 2nd most used metal after steel. Aluminum is one of the lightest metals in the world. Metal is highly conductive of electricity and has soft nature so can be bend without breaking as a result it is used widely in the production of multiple products throughout the world. Naturally, Aluminum is found in an ore called "bauxite" thus bauxite is the basic raw material used in the Aluminum manufacturing process. Among all the industries, Aluminum industry is perhaps youngest. Aluminum was discovered only in 1886. Although bauxite, the principal ore of Aluminum, is abundant all over the earth's crust, its concentration of sizable amount is rare. Bauxite is converted into alumina in refineries. According to USGS India's rank is 9th in terms of bauxite reserves in the world. Aluminum is produced by two different methods, the primary production process which involves the conversion of ores to Aluminum and the other is secondary production (recycling) where the Aluminum scrap is recycled to produce Aluminum again. In India primary Aluminum industry is dominated by 3 companies: Hindalco and Vedanta which are privately owned and National Aluminum Company Ltd. (NALCO) which is a public sector undertaking having a Navratna status.

First attempt to manufacture Aluminum in India was started when Aluminum Corporation of India (ACI) was formed in 1937. But its first venture to produce Aluminum was delayed. Meanwhile, Indian Aluminum Company (IAC) started its production at Aluminum in Kerala. To give a moral as well as financial boost to the industry, the Government announced in 1940 several facilities including import tax exemption and imposition of heavy duty on imported Aluminum. Finally, Aluminum Corporation of India was able to start its production at Jaykeynagar. In 1958, Hindustan Aluminum Corporation (HAC) was incorporated. This company constructed a giant plant at Renukot in Uttar Pradesh which started production in 1962. Subsequently new plants were set up at Mettur of Madras (1965) in the name of Madras Aluminum Company and in the same year Bharat Aluminum Company Limited (BALCO) was established in public sector. Plants of BALCO are situated in Korba of Madhya Pradesh, Ratnagiri in Maharastra and Ambikapur of Chattisgarh. In 1981 National Aluminum Company Limited (NALCO) was established in Koraput of Orissa.

But due to the huge demands India has to import a large volume of Aluminum yearly. At the initiation of the First Five Year Plan, total Indian Aluminum production was only 4 thousand tones. Production increased to 18,000 tons in 1960-61. Production surpassed 160,000 tons in 1970-71. Finally, after expansion of the old units and construction of Korba and Angul projects, production crossed the modest total of 350,000 tons in 1988-89. During 2004, production of Aluminum is estimated to be slightly higher than 0.88 million tones, as compared to 0.624 million tons in year 2000. The chronic power shortage disrupted normal production in many plants.

Due to heavy demand of energy in the conversion of alumina from bauxite, it was not possible to raise the production, despite massive bauxite reserves in the country. Special care had been taken to improve hydel-power projects for the development of Aluminum industry as hydel-power is much cheaper and economic than any other form of energy. Despite massive increase of Aluminum production, overall performance of Indian Aluminum industry is not at all Satisfactory. Since inception, the industry had to overcome several problems. The major problems among these are lower productivity, high cost of energy, uneconomic size of the plants, lack of good quality raw materials, etc. To overcome these difficulties, production cost of Aluminum should be reduced drastically, modern methods of alumina reduction should be introduced and plant-size must be made economically viable.

Recycling of Aluminum products is being emphasized as a facilitator of future growth of the industry. Products such as cans, Aluminum foils, plates and automotive components can be easily recycled thereby saving energy and reducing greenhouse emissions; it is interesting to note that more than 63% of all Aluminum cans are recycled worldwide. Recycling of Aluminum uses only 5% of the energy required for primary production and emits only 5% of the greenhouse gases.

CEMENT INDUSTRY:

Cement is a substance used for building construction that sets, hardens and adheres to other materials by binding them together. Cement is seldom used single; cement is used with other fine material like sand and gravels to produce concrete. India is the second largest producer of cement in the world. India's cement industry is a vital part of its economy, providing employment to more than a million people, directly or indirectly. It was deregulated in 1982; the cement industry has attracted huge investments, both from Indian as well as foreign investors since then. India economy is at boost and the country has a lot of potential for further development due to recent major initiatives as development of smart cities, developing real estate and housing sector, construction and infrastructure sector are all going to benefit the cement industry in India. Several foreign based companies are investing in the country. Availability of the raw materials for making cement, such as limestone and coal are essential for development of cement industry.

The housing sector is the biggest consumer of cement and generates huge demand, accounting for about 67 per cent of the total consumption of cement in India. The other major consumers of cement are infrastructure sector by 13 per cent, commercial construction at 11 per cent and industrial construction sector at 9 per cent. India's total cement production capacity was nearly 425 million tonnes, as of September 2017. The growth of cement industry is expected to be 6-7 per cent in 2017 because of growing housing sector and the government's focus on huge infrastructural development. The per capita consumption of cement is around 225 kg/ person and expected to rise in near future. A huge concentration of cement plants can be seen in the states of Andhra Pradesh, Rajasthan and Tamil Nadu as of 210 large cement plants, 77 are located in these states.

Due to the growing demand, increased construction and infrastructural activities, the cement sector in India is seeing numerous investments and developments in recent. According to data released by the Department of Industrial Policy and Promotion (DIPP), cement and gypsum have attracted Foreign Direct Investment (FDI) worth US$ 5.25 billion between April 2000 and December 2017. In order to help the private sector companies thrive in the industry, the government has been approving their investment schemes. In of Budget 2018-19, Government of India announced setting up of an Affordable Housing Fund of Rs 25,000 crore under the National Housing Bank (NHB) thus it is expected that it will boost the demand of cement from the housing sector.

India is the second largest cement producer in the world and accounts for 6.9 per cent of world's cement output. It is expected that due to the increased demand in housing, commercial construction and industrial construction, cement industry is expected to reach 550-600 million tonnes per annum (MTPA) by the year 2025.

Agro Based Industry (Cotton Textile, Jute textile, Sugar Industry)

COTTON TEXTILE:

India is one of the important cotton-manufacturing countries of the world. Both short- staple and long-staple cotton is grown in the country. Cotton textile industry is an important, ancient and largest organized industry of India. Lakhs of peoples are directly engaged in cotton industry and also lakhs of peoples are indirectly supporting and in response supported by the cotton textile industry in India. Cotton growers, power loom and hand loom operators, traders etc. indirectly gain livelihood from cotton industry. India ranks second in cotton textile manufacturing in the world. The textile industry in India traditionally, after agriculture, is the only industry that has generated huge employment for both skilled and unskilled labour and accounts for a large portion of the total industrial output in the country each year.

Even 5000 years in the past, fine quality cotton textiles were weaved in India. Traces are available from Mohenjo-Daro and Harappa. The cotton textile industry in India was initiated with the establishment of the first cotton textile factory at Fort Gloster near Kolkata in 1818. However, it was closed very soon due to the shortage of raw material. Actual development of the cotton industry started after 1854 when cotton textile mill was established by Kawas Ji Davor in Mumbai; which is located in the cotton growing region of Western India. Since then there has been rapid growth of the industry around Mumbai and Ahmadabad. In 1939 there were 389 cotton textile mills in India. But after the partition of country, about 48% cotton producing area and 15 large cotton textile mills went to Pakistan which was a setback to cotton textile industry in India. After independence serious steps were taken to regenerate the cotton textile industry.

The textile industry continues to be the second-largest employment generating sector in India. It is offering direct employment to over 35 million peoples in the country. The share of textiles in total exports was 11.04% during April–July 2010. In 2010, there were 2,500 textile weaving factories and 4,135 textile finishing factories in all of India. India exports yarn to different countries of the world. Cotton textile industry of India is now in a position to meet the total demand for textiles in the domestic market and with a sufficient surplus for foreign export. India ranks among the largest producer and exporter of cotton textile products. India exports cotton textiles to the countries of Russia, UK, USA, Australia, Sri Lanka, Iran, Germany, Belgium, Italy, etc.

Concentration of Cotton textile centers:

Major factors for the growth of the industry of cotton textile are easy availability of local raw cotton, availability of cheap hydel-power, humid climate required for spinning of the yarn, large capital invested, locally available cheap and skilled labor, good demand for cotton garments and, well-knit transport system etc. Main four regions of cotton textile concentration in India are as:

- **Western Region:** Gujarat and Maharashtra are the most advanced states of this region. Mumbai in Maharashtra and Ahmadabad in Gujarat are two principal centers of this region. Ahmadabad is known as the 'Manchester of India'. The other important cotton textile centers include Nagpur, Pune, Jalgaon, and Sholapur in Maharashtra and Surat, Bharuch, Vadodara, Bhavnagar, Rajkot in Gujarat state.
- **Southern Region:** In Southern India cotton textile mills are located mainly in the states of Tamil Nadu, Kerala, Karnataka and Andhra Pradesh. Important centers of cotton industry are Madurai, Salem, Tiruchirapalli Chennai, Guntur, Mysore, Pondicherry etc. Coimbatore is the largest cotton textile center of Southern region.
- **Northern Region:** This region includes the states of Uttar Pradesh, Delhi, Punjab, Haryana and Rajasthan. The principal centers of this region are Kanpur, Delhi, Amritsar, Ludhiana, Agra etc.
- **Eastern Region:** This region includes the states of West Bengal, Bihar, Orissa and Assam. Maximum mills are concentrated in Kolkata, Sodepur, Belgharia, Shyamnagar, Ghusuri, Salkia, Shrirampur, and Maurigram etc.

Problems associated with the cotton textile industry:

1. Long staple cotton is not well grown in many parts of India.
2. Old machinery.
3. High cost of advanced machinery.
4. The high cost of production.
5. Heavy competition from synthetic fibers like polyester, etc.
6. Huge competition in the world trade from Japan, China, Bangladesh, and UK, etc.
7. Poor modernization of cotton industry.

8. Lack of capital.
9. Problems of skilled and unskilled labors.
10. Poor supply of electricity and inadequate water availability.

The old plant and machinery have to be replaced and introduction of the modernized machinery, easy loan facility, assured availability of raw-materials, labor, and power would ensure balanced growth of cotton industry in India.

JUTE TEXTILE:

Jute industry is an important and organized industry of India. More than 3 lakh direct and 4 lakh indirect employments are generated by jute industry in India. Jute Products have an important place in exported goods from India and country earns crores of rupees of income yearly and the value increasing continuously. In India jute is known as 'Golden Fiber'. Earlier very few products were manufactured from jute but presently a good range of products like curtains, mats, blankets, water proof clothes are manufactured from jute. Jute industry is an ancient industry of India, developed as cottage and household industry in eastern India. The first attempt to modernized jute mill was done by George Oakland at the bank of Hugli River at Rishra in 1855. In 1859 Borneo Jute Company was setup by George Henderson, till 1900 there were 36 jute mills in the region. Both the two world wars created huge demand of jute products. At that time more than 3 lakh workers were engaged directly or indirectly in jute industry and in 1947, 110 jute mills and 68 thousand looms were there in the country. But the division of country proved a great setback to the jute industry as major jute producing area about $(2/3^{rd})$ was now in Bangladesh (Eastern Pakistan).

In 1949 Central Jute Committee was formed. Different five years plans also supported jute industry a lot. Presently, more than 114 jute mills are in India and among them 6 are under the ownership of National Jute Production Nigam. Jute mills are mainly concentrated in the states of West Bengal; and state hold the monopoly in jute production. Other jute producing states are Uttar Pradesh, Andhra Pradesh, Chhattisgarh, Orissa, Bihar and Assam. In the year 2004-05, about 1615.4 thousands metric tons jute were produced in India. India export jute and jute products to USA, UK, Australia, Canada and many African countries. Jute industry of India is facing several problems like heavy competition from China and Bangladesh. Old and traditional and inefficient jute mills, decreasing demands of cabas, bags and jute products, use of manmade fibers etc. are other major problems.

SUGAR INDUSTRY:

Sugar is a daily need commodity in each and every Indian house. India is the world's largest producer of sugarcane and second largest producer of sugar after Cuba. Sugar is produced mainly from sugarcane, and sugarbeet. But in India, sugarcane is the main source of sugar. At present, sugar industry is the second largest agro-based industry of India only after cotton textile industry. If 'gur' and 'khandsari' are also included then India becomes the largest producer. Industry involves a total capital investment of about Rs. 1,250 crore and provides employment to

2.86 lakh workers and about 2.50 crore sugarcane farmers also get benefit from sugar industry. India is rightly called the homeland of sugar and has a long tradition of manufacturing sugar from very past. References of sugar making are found even in the 'Atharva Veda' in the form of 'gur' and 'khandsari'. But modem sugar industry came into existence in India only in the middle of the 19th century, and was introduced by the Dutch in North Bihar in about 1840, unfortunately, attempt was failed. The first successful attempt was made by the indigo planters at the initiative of the British in 1903. In 2009-10 about 744 sugar production plants were functional in the country.

Sugar industry in India is based mainly on sugarcane. Sugarcane is a heavy, low value, weight losing and perishable raw material and cannot be stored for a long time and also cannot be transported over long distances because increased transportation cost would raise the cost of production and the sugarcane may get dry up on the way. Normally, about 100 tonnes of sugarcane is required to produce about 10-12 tonnes of sugar. Therefore, the sugar industries in India are established and concentrated in the areas of sugarcane cultivation. It is clear that sugar industry has two major areas of concentration in India; one comprises Uttar Pradesh, Bihar, Haryana and Punjab region in the north and the other region is that of Maharashtra, Karnataka, Tamil Nadu and Andhra Pradesh in the south.

Regional Distribution of sugar industries:

Firstly in India, sugar industry was developed in Northern states like Uttar Pradesh and Bihar due to various advantages like fertile alluvial soil, extensive plane surface, and lower amount of irrigation, cheap irrigation and coal from Jharkhand and Chhattisgarh and thermal power from Rihand project, Dense population cheap lobours and developed transport network is also helpful in location of these industries in north. Bagasse from sugarcane are also used as fuel. But production of sugar cane is lower as compare to southern states. Southern states on the other side have the advantages of favorable climate, black lava soil, and long duration of crushing and higher contents of sucrose.

Major sugar industries concentrated in the following states of India are:

Uttar Pradesh:

Uttar Pradesh is the traditional producer of sugarcane and sugar; presently it occupies the second rank among the major sugar producing states in India. Uttar Pradesh has more sugar mills than Maharashtra but they are of comparatively smaller size and yield less production. Here more than 100 sugar plants are located. There are two different regions of sugar production in Uttar Pradesh. One region is Basti, Gorakhpur, Gonda, and Deoria in eastern Uttar Pradesh and the other lies in the upper Ganga Plain of western Uttar Pradesh consisting of Saharanpur, Shamli, Deoband, Bulandshahar, Muzaffarnagar, Bijnore, Meerut, and Moradabad. Presently, state accounts for about 24 per cent of the total production of sugar in India.

Maharashtra:

Maharashtra is presently the largest producer of sugar in India. Huge production of sugarcane, higher rate of recovery and longer crushing period are some of the factors which have helped the state to occupy this enviable position. The major concentration of sugar mills in Maharashtra is found in the river valleys in the western part of the Maharashtra Plateau. Ahmednagar is the largest center. The other major centers are in the districts of Kolhapur, Solapur, Satara, Pune and Nashik etc.

Tamil Nadu:

Tamil Nadu has shown phenomenal progress with regard to sugar production in India during the last few years. Positive conditions like favorable climate, high per hectare production of sugarcane, higher sucrose content, high recovery rate and long crushing season have enabled Tamil Nadu to develop its sugar industry at fullest. State has set the mark of highest yield of 9.53 tonnes of sugar per hectare in the whole of India. Most of sugar mills of the state are located in the Coimbatore, North Arcot Ambedkar, South Arcot Vallalur and Tiruchchirapalli.

Karnataka:

Karnataka has more than 30 mills producing about 1,151 thousand tonnes i.e., more than 6 per cent of the total sugar of India. Belgaum and Mandya districts of Karnataka have the highest concentration of sugar mills.

Bijapur, Bellary, Shimoga and Chittradurga are the other districts where sugar mills are scattered.

Andhra Pradesh:

Andhra Pradesh has more mills than the neighboring state of Karnataka but produces only 6.01 per cent of India's sugar. The sugar mills of Andhra Pradesh are comparatively smaller. Majority of the sugar mills are concentrated in East and West Godavari, Krishna, Vishakhapatnam, Nizamabad, Medak and Chittoor districts.

Besides these, sugar is produced in the states of Gujarat, Haryana, Bihar, etc. In Gujarat 16 mills are scattered in the districts of Surat, Bhavnagar, Amreli, Banaskantha, Junagarh, Rajkot and Jamnagar districts. The state produces about 5.56 per cent of the total sugar produced in India. Haryana has only 8 mills located in Rohtak, Ambala, Panipat, Sonipat, Kamal, Faridabad and Hissar districts. Punjab has a total of 13 mills which are located in Amritsar, Jalandhar, Gurdaspur, Sangrur, Patiala and Rupnagar districts. Bihar was the second largest sugar producing state, next to Uttar Pradesh till mid- 1960s. But presently state has been experiencing sluggish growth. Its 28 mills are spread in the districts of Darbhanga, Saran, Champaran and Muzaffarpur, etc. Madhya Pradesh (8 mills in Morena, Gwalior and Shivpuri districts), Rajasthan (5 mills in Ganganagar, Udaipur, Chittaurgarh and Bundi districts), Kerala, Orissa, West Bengal and Assam are the other sugar producer states.

Problems of Sugar Industry:

Sugar industry in India is facing severe and complicated problems which need abrupt attention and coherent solutions. Some of the burning problems of sugar industry in India are briefly described as under:

- Per hectare low yield of sugarcane.
- Short crushing season.
- Unstable production trends.
- Low recovery rate.
- Competition with the 'Khandsari' and 'Gur' making.
- Regional imbalances in distribution of sugar industry.
- Low per capita consumption of sugar.
- High production cost.
- Small and uneconomic size of mills.
- Old and obsolete machinery.
- Poor water and power supply.

- Labour problems.
- Import of sugar by Indian government.
- Huge debts on sugar mills.
- Poor quality of sugarcane.
- Lack of storage, and transportation facilities.
- Poor and delayed payments to the farmers.

Forest Based Industries

India is one among few fastest growing forest-based industries in the world. Forests provide us different types of raw materials which are used in forest based industries. For instance, paper industry, match industry, plywood, furniture, silk industry, lack industry, rayon, resin, leather tanning, sports goods and handicraft industry are some forest based industries.

PAPER INDUSTRY

Paper is one among few daily used products. Use of paper is considered as an important indicator of development of any country. Per person use of paper in India is very low (only 7 kg/person) as compared to world average which is about 50 kg per person. The first effort to produce paper by modern techniques was done in 1812 when a paper mill was established in Serampur of West Bengal. In 1870 Bally Paper Mill was established near Kolkata. The first successful paper mill was set up in 1879 in Lucknow. Again, in 1882, paper mill was set up in Titagarh in West Bengal. Till 1900 there were 7 paper mills in India.

After independence India witnessed a huge development in paper industry. Paper industry is a weight losing industry and about two and half tonnes raw materials are needed for making one tone of paper. The localization of this industry is seen mainly in the areas of raw materials. The main factors that favor the location of the paper industry are the availability of raw materials like soft wood, bamboo, bagasse, rags; various chemicals are also required. Power and adequate supply of soft and clean water and nearness to centers of consumption are important for paper and cardboard industry. India has very little softwood; it depends largely on bamboo, sabai grass, bagasse, straw, waste paper and subabul wood. Bamboo is mostly used raw material for making paper in India and about 70% raw material for paper industry is obtained from bamboo. Karnataka, and Assam are the major producers of bamboo, sabai grass provides 15% raw material and Madhya Pradesh, Maharashtra, Andhra Pradesh and Orissa are the major sabai grass producing states. Bagasse, an important raw material of paper industry, is a sugarcane residue provides 7% pulp for paper industry mainly industrial paper, hard board paper, packing paper etc. are made from it. Besides this, paper pulp is also made from wastepaper and rags. It is used to make handmade paper. India is the leading producer of handmade paper and also a big exporter of handmade paper.

Besides all these straw of paddy, wheat and maize are also used in making of paper. Presently India have more than 700 paper and pulp mills which are producing 58 lakh tonnes of paper and cardboard and 7.7 lakh tonnes of newsprint but the production potentials are much higher. West Bengal, Andhra Pradesh, Maharashtra, Karnataka, Madhya Pradesh, and Uttar Pradesh are the leading producer of paper and cardboard in India. Besides these Tamil-Nadu, Bihar, Haryana and Assam also produce paper and cardboard in significant amount.

NEWSPRINT:

Newsprint production was started by National Newsprint and Paper Mills (NEPA Ltd.) in 1955 at Nepanagar in Madhya Pradesh. Till 1981, it was the only mill in the country manufacturing the newsprint. From 1981-1987, three more newsprint mills were set up at Mysore in Karnataka, Nellore of Andhra Pradesh, and Pugalure in Tamil Nadu. There are about 26 newsprint mills in the India. Among them four large public sector mills namely, National Newsprint and Paper Mills Ltd (NEPA Ltd.), Nepanagar, Madhya Pradesh, Hindustan Newsprint Ltd. (HNL) Kottayam Kerala; Mysore Paper Mills Ltd (MPML), Bhadravati (Karnataka); and Tamil Nadu Newsprint and Paper Ltd. (TNPL) in Kagithapuram of Tamil Nadu are important to mention here.

PROBLEMS OF PAPER INDUSTRY:

There are various problems linked with the paper industry in India. The most serious is the problem of lack of raw material for producing good quality paper and newsprint. Many of the chemicals used by the industry have to be imported. The problem of power shortage is also there with some mills. Several types of assistance have been provided by the government to this industry and it is still fulfilled through import of both paper and pulp.

LAC INDUSTRY:

Lac is used in manufacturing of polish, gramophone records, wood turning, printing ink, paints and varnishes, photographic equipment, bangles, toys and in enameling, as insulating agent and in adhesives. Lac is obtained from an insect named *Cerria Lacca* which secretes a resin and cultivated mainly in India and Thailand. Lac insect lives on trees like pipal, palash, babool, kusum etc. Lac is an important forest product of India. Till 1950, India had most probably monopoly in the production of lac in the world but slowly its position has declined. Lac in India is produced mainly in Madhya Pradesh, Jharkhand, Chhattisgarh, Meghalaya, Assam, Orissa, Uttar Pradesh and West Bengal etc. Chota-Nagpur Plateau is the biggest lac producing region of the India and more than 80% lac produced in India is exported. India is exporter of lac and lac products to USA, Russia, UK, Germany, Italy, Japan, Sweden, Australia, Brazil and France etc. India is a leading country in lac production and 60% of lac in the world is produced here.

RUBBER INDUSTRY:

Rubber is obtained naturally, synthetically and from reclaimed rubber and a range of goods are manufactured from them. Rubber is gaining increasing importance in every aspect of life. At present life of peoples are heavily depending on rubber and rubber goods. The beginning of the rubber industry is traced back to the year 1920 when a rubber goods factory named Dixie Aye Rubber Factory was started in Kolkata. Later on in 1933, Bata Shoe Company and in 1935 Dunlop Rubber Company was started.

The major rubber goods produced by the industry are tyres and tubes of automobiles from heavy trucks to bicycles, surgical gloves, sports goods, footwear, cots, aprons etc. Total production of natural rubber was 774,000 tonnes and average yield was 1,443 tonnes/ hectare in 2014-15. India imports a huge amount of rubber; import of rubber was 442,130 tonnes in 2014-

15. Consumption of rubber is very high in India due to the growing automobile and domestic uses of rubber. The development of automobile industry has considerably increased the demand for tyres and tubes in the country. Natural rubber is found in mainly three states of Kerala, Karnataka and Tamil Nadu. Main centers of rubber industry are Kolkata, Howrah, Mumbai, Shahaganj, Thiruvananthapuram etc. The role of synthetic rubber has increased with the increase in demand of natural rubber. The first synthetic rubber factory was started in Bareilly in 1955. Export of rubber goods is also increasing continuously; UK, Czech Republic, Iraq, Sudan, Korea, are the importer of automobiles tyres whereas USA, Russia, Canada, Middle east purchase rubber footwear. And Afghanistan, Ghana, Greece, Romania, Italy import bicycle tyres from India.

LEATHER AND TANNING INDUSTRY:

India has a long tradition of manufacturing leather and leather goods. India was famous for its leather goods from Vedic period. Tanning of leather is very important part of leather industry. The word 'tanning' is generally refers to a variety of processes collectively which change skins and hides into processed leather. India holds first position in livestock in the world thus has a large availability of skins and hides. Industry is running both under organized and unorganized sectors providing employment more than 2.5 million peoples. Leather industry occupies an important place in respect of foreign exchange earnings and employment generation in India. Role of small, cottage, household and artisans are more important in tanning industry as about 72% of the total production comes from them. The first tannary in India established in 1867 in Kanpur to fulfill the military demands. At the time of independence, there were about 32 organized tanneries in India. Tanning of hides and skins and manufacturing of leather goods is concentrated in Kolkata, Agra, Kanpur, Mumbai, Chennai, Coimbatore, Bangalore, Kapurthala, Bhopal, Tonk, Tiruchchirappalli, and Perambur etc. Tamil Nadu has the largest concentration of tanning industries in India.

Leather is used for manufacturing garments, footwear, suitcases, bags, etc. Export from the leather sector today account for around four percent of India's export. Russia, USA, UK, Japan, Italy, Germany, France, Canada and Yugoslavia are buyers of Indian leather and leather goods. Presently industry is facing sever environmental problems and due to courts intervention many small scale industries are at the closing stage as they are not capable of to follow and fulfill the norms of the environment protection laws.

MATCH INDUSTRY:

Match industry in India is important industry because it deals with everyday needs and also is good earner of revenue for the government. Match production in India is done in both modern factories and at cottage and house hold levels. The first match factory in India was established in 1921 in Ahmadabad. The Western India Match Company (WIMCO) came into existence in 1923; it started five factories at Bareilly, Kolkata, Chennai, Ambarnath in Mumbai and in Dhubri of Assam. About 30 per cent match produced in India are by small scale units and cottage industries and rest by the factories of WIMCO along with Assam Match Co. (AMCO.)

i.e. about 70%. There are about one thousand small scale units of match manufacturing.

The matchstick is made by a special kind of soft wood. The woods of the trees called dhoop, didhu, bakota, poplart, salai, mango, semal, sundari etc. is especially used for it. The phosphorus and various other chemicals as paraffin, potash, are still imported. Match factory requires cheap and skilled labor because one-third of the cost of manufacturing match is on labor. This is most localized industry of South India and Maharashtra; Pune, Chinglepet, Tirunelveli, Ramanathpuram, Kolkata, Mumbai, Chandrapur, Thane, Hyderabad, Dhubri, Bilaspur, Jabalpur, Kota, Ahmadabad and Bareilly, Meerut, are the main center of match production in India.

SILK INDUSTRY:

There are two stages in silk industry one is sericulture and obtaining of silk fibers and another one is processing of silk to produce silk textile from silk fibers. Sericulture is completely forest based industry. Sericulture is done mainly on the mulberry trees but the trees like, oak, mahua, castor, sal, plum, kusum etc. are also used for silk worm rearing. More than half of the total silk production in the country is done only in Karnataka. Other major silk producing states are West Bengal, Jharkhand, Jammu & Kashmir, Orissa, and Madhya Pradesh. Several kinds of silk are produced in India for instance:

Mulberry silk: This is the silk made obtained by sericulture on mulberry trees. This is the best kind of silk and 85% of the silk produced in the India is mulberry silk. It is produced in the states like Karnataka (mainly in Bengaluru, Mysore, Kolar and Tumkur districts), West Bengal (Bankura, Murshidabad, Midnapur and Burdwan districts), Assam and Jammu & Kashmir.

Muga silk: This silk is also produced by sericulture done on the mulberry trees and produced mostly done in Assam, West Bengal and Jammu & Kashmir states.

Tasar silk: It is produced by sericulture done on the wild mulberry trees. The major tasar silk producing states are Jharkhand, Orissa and Madhya Pradesh.

Eri silk: It is produced by rearing silk worm done on the leaves of castor and a low quality silk.

Silk Textile Industry: It is indirectly a forest based industry. Silk industry is localized either in the centers of raw material or in the place of demand and or in some industrial cluster. Karnataka is the largest producer of silk fibers in India. About half of the silk fibers in the country are produced by Karnataka alone. Other important centers of silk industry are

Mysore, Bengaluru, Coimbatore and Srinagar, Varanasi, Tirupati, Madurai, Kanjivaram, Bhagalpur (Bihar), Chennai and Mumbai.

BEEDI INDUSTRY:

The beedi making industry has developed mainly in tribal regions. This industry is purely baesd on the forest tree leaves known as 'Tendu'. Madhya Pradesh is the largest producer of beedi because the 'tendu' leaves are found mostly in the forests of this state.

Besides above mentioned industries, several industries related to sandalwood in Karnataka and eucalyptus in Tamil Nadu has developed. The woodcraft industry has developed in Karnataka, Himachal Pradesh and Jammu and Kashmir. Copra (coconut and its fibers) industry (undertaken by the Coconut Board of India) has developed in Kerala.

RAYON INDUSTRY:

Rayon is a manufactured i.e. manmade fiber made from regenerated cellulose fiber. Manmade fibers like rayon are an essential part of textile industry in India. The many types and grades of rayon are produced for making textile in India. Their feel and texture are just like natural fibers such as silk, wool, cotton, and linen etc. Rayon is made from purified cellulose, primarily from wood pulp which is obtained from bamboo and eucalyptus and is converted chemically into a soluble compound. This compound is dissolved and changed into fibers of cellulose. The fibers can be easily dyed in a wide range of colors. Rayon fabrics are very soft, and comfortable thus are in great demand. Till 1935 rayon industry was based on imported fibers. But first indigenous rayon manufacturing mill was established in Travancore of Kerala in 1945 and production started from 1950. After that various rayon industries were established in Mumbai, Hyderabad, and Madhya Pradesh. Presently more than 50 mills are making synthetic fibers and providing yarns to lakhs of power looms and hand looms in India. Largest concentration of rayon industry can be seen in the states of Maharashtra, Uttar Pradesh, Gujarat, West Bengal, Tamil Nadu and Delhi etc. Shortage of raw materials, lack of adequate machinery, labor, and chemicals used, old and traditional machinery, adequate power and water supply are the major problems associated with Indian rayon industry.

RESIN INDUSTRY:

Resin is a sticky, flammable organic substance, generally insoluble in water, obtained by some trees and other plants for instance from fir and pine. A solid or liquid synthetic organic polymer used as the basis of plastics, adhesives, varnishes, or other products.

Household Industry

Household industries are those industries mainly run by the head of the family or with the help of the family members at home or within the village in rural areas. These industries are mainly run as unregistered.

The main norm of a household industry is the participation of one or more members of a family. This criterion applied in urban areas too. There is greater possibility of the members of the family to help in the industry. A household industry is one that is engaged in production, processing, servicing, repairing or making and selling of produced goods. Actually no or very poor mechanization is associated with household industries.

Engineering Industry

Engineering Industry is concerned with the production of a wide range of heavy and light machines and its associated products. They produce machines, engines of automobiles, tractors, harvesters, and other agricultural and mining machines, etc. Engineering industries can be classified into various types depending upon the shape and size of the products, amount of raw materials used and capital invested, and also number of labors engaged in them. There are three main types of engineering industries developed in India are as follows: Heavy Mechanical Engineering Industry, Light Mechanical Engineering Industry, Electrical Engineering Industry.

Engineering industry makes base for the industrialization of any country. The Indian engineering industrial sector is witnessing an extraordinary growth from last few years. The Indian engineering sector is of strategic importance to the Indian economy owing to its intense integration with other industrial segments. The sector has been de-licensed and enjoys 100 per cent FDI. India exports different transport equipment, capital goods, other machinery and equipment and light engineering products such as castings, forgings and fasteners to various countries of the world. Export of engineering goods from India was of Rs. 198 crore in 1970-71 which increased to 433868 crore in 2014-15. But various problems like lack of raw materials, lack of capital, heavy rent, higher competitions, lack of quality control and poor domestic demands are also associated with engineering industries in India. To solve these problems government should provide subsidies, easy means of capital should develop, and measures of quality control are must.

Other Demand-Based Industries

All the industries which cater the needs of the population from daily goods to heavily mechanized goods and services are included in the group of demand based industries.

SUMMARY:

In ancient period India was a developed industrial setup and major production was done in the form of household, cottage and artisan basis. India clothes like muslin, cotton and silk, crafts, artistic wares, were famous and in great demand in the world. But the rule of British and industrial revolution were the hazard for cottage and small scale industries of India. These led to the decay of traditional artisans and handicrafts. Wrong policies of British rulers degraded the Indian small industries.

New era of industrial development started only after the independence of India. Various goals oriented five year plans had provided necessary base of capital, technology, decisions making, execution and co-operation to the industrial rise of India. Presently industries are playing an important role in the development of the country. Industries are providing huge employment to the population of India, higher income, changing the face of Indian economy, facilitating trade and commerce, earning valuable foreign exchange, and strengthening economy. The economy of India is developing as mixed economy and is the world's sixth-largest economy by nominal GDP and the third-largest by purchasing power parity (PPP). After 1991 economic liberalization, India achieved 6-7% average GDP growth annually. India's economy is among few fastest growing economies of the world. Future growth prospective of the Indian economy is very optimistic due to its young population, increasing demands of goods and services.

IT industry, the rising sector of Indian industries, is the largest private-sector employer in India. Industrial sector has stable shares in economic contribution about 26% of GDP in 2013–14. Automobile, e-commerce, health industry, IT industry and BPO, and tourism are growing sectors of Indian economy.

Industrial development is presently considered as the base and prerequisite of modern economic development of the countries. Countries throughout the world are developing its industries and exploring the resource base of theirs. Rapid resource utilization, economic development, upgrading the living standards of populations, and taking benefits of the globalizations are the major goals of the countries. Countries are considered powerful and developed when they have developed industries of all kind for instance iron and steel industry, heavy machinery making, automobile industry, chemical and fertilizer industry, oil and allied products production, artillery production, cement industry, drugs and rubber industry etc. Recently information technology industry, tourism industry, health industry, education industry and entertainment industry have developing rapidly with the changing cultural, economic and demand aspects of the world's populations. There are various more aspects are waiting to be explored.

GLOSSARY:

1. **BPO-** Business Process outsourcing
2. **Industry-** An economic activity which is concerned with the processing of raw materials and manufacturing of goods
3. **Economy-**An economy is the large set of inter-related production and consumption activities that facilitate careful resources management
4. **Mixed economy-** An economic system of combined private and state ventures
5. **Socialist Economy-** Socialist economy means the system where economic system is controlled and regulated by the government so as to ensure public welfare
6. **PPP-** Purchasing power parity **IT-** Information Technology **USD-** United States Dollar **FDI-** Foreign direct investment
7. **Globalization-** the process by which businesses or other organizations start operating on an international scale
8. **Liberalization-** process whereby a state lifts its restrictions and regulations on private individual activities
9. **Hydel-power-** energy generated by the transfer of free-falling water energy to electricity
10. **Industry-** an economic activity that is concerned with the production of goods
11. **E-commerce-** online buying or selling of products

CHECK YOUR PROGRESS:

1. Industry refers to an economic activity that is concerned with the production of goods, extraction of minerals or to provide the services.
2. Industries use raw material obtained from agriculture for processing is known as agro-based industries.
3. Bauxite is the major are used in aluminum industry.
4. TISCO was established by Jamshed ji Tata.
5. SAIL was established in 1974.
6. Aluminum was discovered in 1886.
7. ATC was come into existence in 1937.
8. Frist cotton textile industry in India was established in the year 1818 at Fort Gloster.
9. Nepanagar is famous for Newsprint.
10. Lac is obtained from cerria Lacca insect.
11. Four type of Silks are produced in India.
12. Leaves of Tendu plant are used in Bidi industry.
13. Cottage Industry run by the family head or by the members of the family in home.
14. E-commerce, health industry, IT industry, BPO, and tourism are growing sectors of Indian economy.

REFERENCES:

1. Arnold, David. (2004). *The New Cambridge History of India: Science, Technology and Medicine in Colonial India*, Cambridge University Press.
2. Balasubramaniam, R. (2002). *Delhi Iron Pillar: New Insights*, Indian Institute of Advanced Studies.
3. Gommans, Jos J. L. (2002). *Mughal Warfare: Indian Frontiers and Highroads to Empire, 1500-1700*, Rutledge.
4. Mamoria, Chaturbhuj. (1992): "Adhunik Bharat ka Brihat Bhoogol", Sahitya Bhavan, Agra.
5. Ojha, S.S. "Bharat ka Bhoogol". (2005): Bhaugolik Adhyan Sansthan, Govindpur, Allahabad.
6. Rakesh Tewari, 2003, *The origins of iron-working in India: new evidence from the CentralGanga Plain and the Eastern Vindhyas.*
7. Srinivasan, S. & Ranganathan, S., *Wootz Steel: An Advanced Material of the Ancient World*, Indian Institute of Science.

8. Tiwari, R.C. (2003):"Geography of India", Prayag Pustak Bhawan, Allahabad.

9. Agriculture Survey of India, 2017-18.

10. Economic Survey of India (vol.1st and 2nd). Oxford University Press, New Delhi.

11. Gopalakrishnan, R. "Geography of India", Jawahar Publishers.

12. Indian Budget, 2017-18.

13. Industrial Survey of India, 2107-18.

14. Sen Gupta, P. (1968). Economic Regionalization of India, Census of India Publication.

15. Singh, Jagdish. (2003). "India: A Comprehensive Systematic Geography", Gyanodaya Prakashan, Gorakhapur.

16. Singh, L.R. (ed.). (1987): "India: A Regional Geography", New Printindia Pvt. Ltd., Ghaziabad, U.P.

TERMINAL QUESTIONS:

A. Long Questions

1. What do you understand by industry? Explain major types of industries with examples?

2. Describe Iron and steel industry of India in detail with problems prevailed and solutions?

3. What do you mean by agro-based industry? Explain two of them?

4. What are the major forests based industries? Write notes on three of them?

5. Explain cement industry of India with their distribution, problems and solutions?

B. Short Questions

1. What do you mean by industry?

2. What do you mean by agro-based industries?

3. Name the major ore used in aluminum industry?

4. Who established TISCO?

5. When SAIL was established?

6. In which year aluminum was discovered?
7. In Which year AIC was came into existence?
8. When and where first cotton textile industry in India was established?
9. Why Nepanagar is famous for?
10. Name the insect from which lac is obtained from?
11. How many type of silk is produced in India?
12. Name the plant whose leaves are used in bidi industry?
13. What do you mean by cottage industry?
14. Name few rising sector of Indian industry?

C. Multiple choice questions

1. Raw material based industries include?

1. Agro industries
2. Wooden Industries
3. Ocean basis industries
4. All of the above

(Answer- 4)

2. Industries are divided on the basis of size. 1- 2

1. 4
2. 6
3. 8

(Answer- 1)

3. Includes division of industries on the basis of ownership.

1. Private Sector
2. State Owned Public
3. Joint Industries
4. All of the above

(Answer- 4)

4. When and who established the modern iron industry.

1. 1907 Jamsd ji Tata
2. 1954 Dawer ji Kavas
3. 1919 IISCO
4. None of the Above

(Answer - 1)

5. These are the major problems of the iron and steel industry.

1. Procurement of quality raw materials
2. Lack water supply
3. Lack of power supply
4. All of the above

(Answer - 4)

6. When was the production of aluminum started for the first time in India?

1. ACI 1937
2. TISCO 1907
3. ISCO 1919
4. All of the above

(Answer 1)

7. Full form of NHB?

1. National Housing Bank
2. New House Bank
3. Nuclear House Board
4. None of the Above

(Answer- 1)

8. Agro based industry is?

1. Cotton
2. Textile, Jute
3. Sugarcane
4. all of the above

(Answer-4)

9. The first cotton industry was established in India.

1. 1818
2. 1854
3. 1860
4. 1994

(Answer - 2)

10. What are the main problems of jute industry?

1. Old machine
2. The high cost of production
3. Lack of Capital
4. All of the above

(Answer - 4)

The Co-author Dr Vivek Sidhu

Dr. Vivek Sidhu is a distinguished academician and legal scholar, currently serving Director at the School of Law, Sabarmati University. Born on August 19, 1985, in Gujarat, Dr. Vivek Sidhu brings with him an extensive academic background in law, particularly in the areas of Criminal Law, Research Methodology, and Constitutional Law. He earned his Ph.D. in Law in 2022 from Madhav University, Rajasthan, where his research focused on the legal provisions against female foeticide in India, with a special emphasis on the state of Gujarat.

Dr. Vivek Sidhu has contributed significantly to legal scholarship, having published research papers in renowned international and national journals on topics such as the status of women, female foeticide, and juvenile justice. His research papers have appeared in esteemed publications like NIU International Journal of Human Rights and Anveshak. He has also actively participated in various seminars and conferences at the international, national, and state levels, presenting papers on critical socio-legal issues, including the Uniform Civil Code and juvenile justice.

With over six years of teaching experience, Dr. Vivek Sidhu has served as a Ph.D. guide and course coordinator. He is involved in curriculum development and has played a key role in university administration, including managing exams and guiding the academic development of law programs. His commitment to education and research is complemented by his hobbies of reading and sharing knowledge, which reflect his passion for teaching and engaging with students.

A multi-linguist fluent in Gujarati, Hindi, English, and Punjabi, Dr. Vivek Sidhu is also an avid chess player and has a deep interest in promoting women's rights and empowerment through his academic work and public engagements.

This book "Urbanization and Rural Dynamics in India" is the first book which has launched Dr Vivek Sidhu as a published international author.

The Author Dr Anshumali Pandey

Professor (Dr) Anshumali Pandey

Meet the remarkable Dr. Anshumali Pandey, a living testament to excellence in education, hospitality, tourism, and the fascinating world of tribal food. A true polymath, he effortlessly wears the hats of a seasoned educator, esteemed chef, celebrated author, meticulous business auditor, and adventurous culinary traveller.

With a focus on higher education, office administration, HR, labor laws, audit, procurement, and tender processes, Dr. Pandey has gained prominence as a leading hospitality educator, holding a distinguished PhD in the field.

Fuelling his passion for tribal food, tourism, and village exploration, he has delved deep into extensive research, leading to numerous illuminating research papers and publications. Notably, the Ministry of Tourism, Government of India, recognized his expertise and contributions, bestowing upon him a National Appreciation certificate and a cherished memento in 2018.

Drawing from a rich experience spanning over 26 years in the professional realm, Dr. Anshumali Pandey has honed the art of precise and compelling writing. This has resulted in an impressive collection of 96 publications, comprising 75 enlightening books and captivating short stories. His literary repertoire covers a wide spectrum, ranging from culinary expertise to HR mastery, from nurturing young minds through children's books to exploring the realms of spirituality.

Residing with his family in the picturesque Western Indian tribal belt of the union territory of Dadra & Nagar Haveli for more than two decades, Dr. Pandey has wholeheartedly dedicated his time to understanding and aiding the tribal and rural communities of the region. His writings not only showcase his immense expertise but also reflect his profound knowledge of diverse subjects he has thoughtfully chosen for his books.

A true champion of the hospitality sector, Dr. Anshumali Pandey's multifaceted prowess has established him as a reputable and revered name in the industry. His boundless passion and unwavering commitment make him an inspiring figure for aspiring professionals across various fields.

Books written by the Author are –

1. Theory of Indian Cookery
2. Beauty and Irony of Silvassa Tourism
3. A Short Indian Food Story
4. Be Your Own Guide to Indian Cuisine
5. Cookery Fundamentals
6. History of Indian Food (2 Editions Printed)
7. The Great Indian Story Book for Children
8. Personal Budget: Easy Work Book
9. Online Classes Log Book
10. Dictionary Making Work Book for School Children
11. The Lazy Bed
12. Hindu Dharm (हिन्दू धर्म) (In Hindi Language)
13. Where is my coffee?
14. Your First Job is Never your Last (Volume 1)
15. You are Almost There (Quick Fix Resume and Interview Hacks)
16. Working for the Enemy? - A lesson in Career Management
17. Public Speaking for the Young
18. A Date With Coffee
19. How to be The Best Hotel Front Office Employee
20. Diploma in Food Production, The complete Syllabus
21. Diploma in F&B Service, The Complete Syllabus
22. Diploma in Front Office, The Complete Syllabus
23. The Time to Speak is Now

24. Munshi Premchand (Short Stories in English)
25. The Housekeeping Department, Text Book
26. Hitchhiker's Guide to Trekking in Uttarakhand
27. Uttarakhand, A divine Land for a Reason
28. Bachhon ke liye rochak kahaniyan (बच्चों के लिए रोचक कहानियाँ) (In Hindi Language)
29. Basic Communication Skills of English
30. The Basic Office Organisation Book for Start-ups
31. Hospitality HRM
32. Hospitality Marketing
33. Bakery Ingredients and Tools
34. Human Resource Management for Indian Professionals
35. The process of LAWFULLY operating a Hospitality business in India
36. Indian Classical Sweets: History, Tradition and Recipes
37. History of India's Himalayan Cuisine: Classical Cookery of Kashmir, Laddakh, Jammu, Himachal, Lahaul, Spiti, Garhwal, Kumaon.
38. Vindu: Andhra Cuisine (Part 1 of South Indian Trilogy)
39. Saappadu: Tamil Cuisine (Part 2 of South Indian Trilogy)
40. Sadya: Malayali Cuisine (Part 3 of South Indian Trilogy)
41. South Indian Cuisine - The Researcher's Guide Book
42. The Ramayana for Children and other short stories from Indian Mythology
43. Legends of the Tribal Shiva
44. Third Generation Children's Story Book
45. It's Elementary: The Top Nine Adventures from the memoirs of Dr John H Watson
46. UNITY IN DIVERSITY, The foundation of Indian Tourism
47. The Thar Express: Culinary History of Rajasthan and Gujarat
48. Basics of Computerized Accounting
49. Impact (Impact of Globalization on Indian Social Life)
50. Vishnu – The Lord of Amazing Incarnations
51. Being a Mahatma in the Freedom Struggle
52. The Culinary Journey of Purvanchal: Lucknow to Patna
53. Culinary History of the Gangetic Plains
54. Indian Culinary Secrets
55. The Story of Jain and Parsi Food
56. The Great Indian Pilgrimage Tourism
57. Introduction to Tourism Studies – Text Book

58. Bread and Rolls
59. Diploma in Digital Marketing the Complete Syllabus
60. The Theory of Sweetened Bakery Foods
61. Campus Placement Guide for Management Trainee in Leading Hotels
62. Diploma in Housekeeping Management, the Complete Syllabus
63. Jokes and Stories for Kids
64. Demigods of India
65. Practical Cookery Guide Book for Parents and School Teachers
66. Introduction to Cookery for Elementary School Children (Kindle)
67. The Fearless Entrepreneur (Being your own Boss)
68. Culinary Heritage of Bengal's Widow Culture
69. Journey into the Mythological Wisdom of Vedas & Puranas
70. From Stigma to Strength: The Legacy of Bengal's Widowhood
71. HAKKA: Discovering a Vibrant Community in India
72. The Indo Chinese Pot Boiler
73. Bombay Daak: *Discovering the Kolis of the Seven Islands*
74. Speak Your Mind: A Guide to Clear and Impactful Communication
75. Urbanization And Rural Dynamics In India

Connect with me: anshumali.pandey@gmail.com
https://notionpress.com/author/337004

Please scan this QR code on your phone to know more about the latest and complete works of Dr Anshumali Pandey